Murder for Breakfast

The True Story of Alma Petty Gatlin and the Preacher Who Betrayed Her

Phil Link

 Down Home Press, Asheboro, N.C.

ISBN 1-878086-94-4

Library of Congress Control Number: 2002106145

Printed in the United States of America

Book design by Beth Hennington

Cover design by Tim Rickard

Down Home Press
P.O Box 4126
Asheboro, N.C. 27204

Distributed by:
John F. Blair, Publisher
1406 Plaza Dr.
Winston-Salem, N.C. 27103

To the memory of my parents,

Henry Ernest "H.E." Link
and Corrinna Lewis Link

Other Books by Phil Link

Another Time
Nobody Left to Ask

INTRODUCTION

Involvement with a murder, however peripheral, leaves a lasting impression. Thus it was for my friend Phil Link, who at age eleven watched through a basement window as the moldering body of a neighbor was unearthed from beneath a coal pile.

The fascination with the murder of Smith Petty, who died from a blow to the head with the blunt end of an ax, would last throughout Phil's long and active lifetime.

I can't now remember how long ago it was when Phil first told me about Alma Petty Gatlin's trial for killing her father and the excitement and nationwide attention it brought to his hometown of Reidsville, N.C., in 1928. Perhaps it was while he was helping me with my book *Bitter Blood*, about a series of horrendous murders that also centered on Reidsville.

But for Phil, a renowned raconteur, the excitement stirred by the telling of the recovery of Smith Petty's body was the same as if it had just occurred, and he had dashed home to tell his family what he had witnessed.

When Phil finally decided to write a book about the Alma Petty Gatlin case, he went at it with an exuberance that belied his years, searching through archives and old newspaper files, seeking out every person who had memories of the long-ago events and the people involved. He brought that same excitement and immediacy to the pages of this book, a book that breathes with Phil's vast knowledge of Reidsville and its people.

In *Murder for Breakfast*, Phil leaves a unique and lasting contribution not only to his hometown but to the lore of murder in the Old North State.

—Jerry Bledsoe

TO THE READER

Being an eyewitness to the discovery of a neighbor's body buried in his own basement could hardly fail to make an indelible impression on a young schoolboy. And today the memory of that bizarre scene still persists, hard and sharp as a flash photo by Weegee.

Seventy-five years later, the tale of the ax murder continues to be passed down from generation to generation. Now, finally, my lifelong dream of getting the story in print is a reality. But it never would have happened without the help and encouragement of my friend Jerry Bledsoe.

Many people in and around Reidsville made valuable contributions. When the word got around 11 years ago that I was working on a book about the murder, I was surprised at the number of people who wanted to help. More people than I can remember came forward with yellowed and crumbling old newspapers rescued from their attics. Other local people, many now dead, generously gave me their time and shared firsthand information. I am grateful to all these people. The full story could not have been told without them. They brought to life a good deal of the material I obtained by researching countless newspaper articles on microfilm. But, more importantly, these people provided a great deal of personal information that had never appeared in print.

Early on in my research, I discovered that no transcript of Alma Petty Gatlin's trial was available. So chapters on the trial are based largely on information gleaned from old newspapers, mainly *The Reidsville Review*, the *Greensboro Daily Record*, and the *Danville Bee*. This blanket acknowledgement seems appropriate, since many of the courtroom scenes are a blend of news stories from different papers.

This true story is told as accurately and honestly as my personal knowledge and considerable research would allow. But in order to bring certain scenes alive, I had to invent dialogue as I imagined it might have been spoken. Although the words are mine, the facts revealed by the imaginary conversations are true. My goal was to entertain the reader while preserving the essence of a given episode.

PREFACE

The last time I saw Smith Petty alive, I was turning one-handed cartwheels in his front yard. Everybody in the neighborhood said the same thing: Philip Link was always up to something, trying to attract somebody's attention. And I'll admit it; I did like to show off. One of my favorite stunts, when I was eleven, was to pretend I was an acrobat in the circus and perform for anybody I thought would watch me. And on that particular day, Mr. Petty and his grown daughter, Alma, who were sitting together in the porch swing, seemed a likely audience. Mr. Petty had one arm draped across the back of the swing and they were talking quietly, not really paying any attention to me. At least, that was the way it looked when I stopped whirling long enough to notice. I was getting tired anyway, so while I was catching my breath, I rehearsed in my mind what I had heard at the Toby tent show. Then I announced in a loud voice: "Ladies and gentlemen, if you enjoyed the show, tell your friends; if you didn't like it, keep your mouth shut." They both laughed and I went on home. I couldn't remember ever hearing Mr. Petty laugh out loud before.

The next time I saw Mr. Petty, almost a year later, I was on my knees, peeping in their basement window, and I heard Sheriff Chunk Smith tell his men to be careful how they dug after they got the coal shoveled out of the way. All of a sudden I smelled this awful odor, way yonder worse than the stink of raw sewage in the stagnant creek down in the holler, where I wasn't supposed to play. The odor coming from the basement had a peculiar smell, so strong it took my breath and made me jerk my head back. There was something putrid down there. I was scared to look, but I looked anyway. After I looked, I wished I hadn't. It was a terrible sight: a dead body, all rotten, crammed in a shallow grave that had been hidden under the coal pile. My stomach started feeling funny, like I was going to throw up. That was when I lit out running, flying across the street as fast as my legs would carry me, heading for home. I had to tell Mama. They had found Mr. Petty.

Smith Petty.
(Sketch by Phil
Link)

Smith Petty's wife,
Janie. (Sketch by
Phil Link)

1

Jimmy Vaughn's thirteenth birthday was just a week and a day away the Saturday morning his daddy, Ed Vaughn, hitched a red horse named Dan to the wagon that would carry them to Reidsville, not quite four miles away. Marshall Hatchett, who lived on the same farm, went with them. He didn't need to go, the black man said, but he appreciated the offer of a ride and believed he would go, just to be going; maybe he'd meet up with somebody in town he hadn't seen lately.

When they got to town and crossed the railroad to South West Market Street, always congested and teeming with people on Saturdays, Marshall hopped off the wagon, said he'd see them later and ambled away, heading north. Ed Vaughn watered his horse at the cement trough near Gillie's Store before driving his wagon up the wooden ramp in back of Pinnix's Warehouse; then he and his son went to Gillie's, where Mr. Vaughn bartered the eggs and live chickens they'd brought in from the country for such staples as sugar, coffee, salt and whatever else might be running low at home. They didn't have to buy flour, since they grew their own wheat and had it ground into flour at Wray's Mill just down the street. Tobacco was their cash crop, but like all farmers in the '20s, they were basically self-sufficient and produced just about everything that was set on the dinner table: from ham and eggs to cornbread, buttermilk, snap beans, and the turnip salad that nobody ever called turnip greens, except a few town folks trying to get above their raising.

Although both Gillie's and Apple's Store were crowded with farmers, nobody was in a hurry to be waited on, and there was much laughing and talking as customers held leisurely conversations with clerks and store owners and with each other. That was part of the pleasure of coming to town on Saturday: Visiting with friends who had common interests in things like making a good crop of tobacco, worrying about not getting enough rain at the right time or about getting too much rain at the wrong time, and always worrying about the threat of blue mold. But their conversations were far from being all gloom-doom; there were jokes and tales told on each other. And there was "Lying John" Burton, who didn't ask to be believed; he asked only to be listened to. And that was never a problem. Lying John always had a good audience for his tall tales, told only to entertain, never to hurt anybody, for he was a humorous man without a malicious bone in his body. He loved people almost as much as he loved to lie, and the more people laughed, the more outlandish his tales became.

Early in the afternoon, a man came into Apple's Store and said it was all over town that Sheriff Chunk Smith had found a dead man buried in somebody's basement on Lindsey Street, just a block from John Watt's Corner. A town boy said he knew where that was and that it wasn't far, so several men and the boy decided to walk over there. Jimmy Vaughn asked his daddy if he could go with them. Mr. Vaughn said he reckoned it would be all right but not to stay all day.

When they got there, the side yard was full of people. The crowd clogged the sidewalk, and many stood in the middle of Franklin Street with no more thought of getting run over by a car than if they were in Fels' cow pasture. The front yard was roped off and a young man was posted at the front door to keep anybody from going inside that way. Sheriff Chunk Smith had pressed into service as a guard sixteen-year-old J. C. Smith, who lived just down the street, next door to the Billy Giles house, where the sheriff and his wife Gladys, a nurse, had rooms upstairs.

Although nobody was allowed inside the house, there was nothing to stop anybody who wanted to go into the basement and see the body, which was not removed from its shallow grave until about four o'clock that afternoon. Jimmy Vaughn and the town boy got in line with the others and they made their way down the slope to the basement door. Jimmy took one look through the door and saw in a blur all he wanted to see: the scattered coal and displaced dirt piled beside the two-foot hole where the decomposed body lay face down. He got out of there.

When Jimmy told his daddy about what he had seen, Ed

Shallow grave in the coal bin where sheriff's deputies discovered the body. (Photo courtesy N.C. Collection, UNC Library at Chapel Hill)

Vaughn said he didn't know what the world was coming to.

Neither father nor son thought anything about it when Marshall Hatchett didn't show up to ride back with them. It wasn't the first time he had stayed on longer and caught a ride on some other farmer's wagon.

It was nearly dark when Marshall walked past their house on his way home. He stopped by to tell them why he was late getting back. "Y'all know what I been doing?" he asked, plainly still excited about something. "Me and another fellow been digging," he announced.

"Digging?" Jimmy's daddy said.

"Yessir, Mister Ed. Digging," answered Marshall, pleased with himself for what he was about to tell them. "And you ain't gonna believe what we was digging for. Lemme explain how everything happened. After I left y'all, I walked on down to the other end of the street, where the pool hall is. But I ain't never set foot inside that place. I just like to go by there and see if I know anybody hanging around outside. The sidewalk where they congregate in front of the pool hall is always crammed full of men and boys laughing and talking every Saturday, unless it's raining. Anyway, I run into this ole boy I hadn't seen in no telling how long, and he was telling me about living in town now. Then I noticed he started looking funny and said he wondered what all them deputy sheriffs was doing down there. One of them was Mister Dick Stokes, he said, and he was the main deputy. Anyway, it turned out that all they wanted was somebody to do some digging. I told them I would go, be glad to pick me up a little piece of money. Another fellow by the name of Dave Bowman said he was a good digger, wouldn't't of worked for Mr. Gladstone so long if he wasn't't. Told me Mr. Gladstone was a plumber, in case I didn't know. Besides digging, Dave said he delivered kerosene oil. Didn't have to tell me that. His overalls smelled like they was made out of kerosene. Anyhow, we both went with them and they put us to work digging in a basement. The sheriff had us shovel some of the coal out of the way first, and when I got to a place where the dirt was softer and kinda loose, I started digging real careful, like they told us. Next thing you know, I'm hollering out that I done struck something! And it was him! That dead man they was looking for. His body was so rotten it looked like it done melted. And his head, it was all bashed in. I don't never want to see nothing like that again, and I sho' don't want to smell nothing that stinks that bad again. It was so strong it plumb covered up Dave's El Reeso cigar, bad as it smelled. Couldn't even smell the kerosene. All I could smell was that dead man. I liked to of throwed up. But I managed not to."

"I know how awful it smelled," Jimmy said. "I went down there."

"When? When was you down there?" Marshall asked, his disappointment showing.

"Y'all must have been gone by the time I got there. The yard was full of folks going up and down the hill, but if I saw the sheriff or any deputies, I didn't know it," Jimmy said.

Marshall grinned. "Well, if you'd of seen me, you'd of seen at least one deputy." The grin broadened. "'Cause they done went and deputized me before I ever started digging."

It was plain to see that Marshall was too tickled over his being deputized to have made the story up.

Peeping unnoticed through the basement window and watching them dig, I was more interested in what they were doing than who they were. But I could have confirmed Marshall's story. One minute he was quietly shoveling, the next minute he let out a little yelp and said he had "done struck something!" I still remember his exact words because he used the word "struck" instead of the more common word "hit."

When they shoveled the dirt out of the way and I saw the body, I started feeling sort of sick. But not sick enough to keep me from running all the way home. It wasn't far. We lived just two houses up the street from the Pettys.

When I told Mama what I had just seen, she said she had to sit down a minute. She shook her head and said that all this time everybody had been wondering where Mr. Petty disappeared to, and he hadn't gone anywhere. The poor man was right there in the basement the whole time. But what she wanted to know was how and why his body got down there.

I told Mama I didn't know and she said of course I didn't. Then as if she had just noticed, she said I looked a little pale and asked if I was all right. I told her I was okay, and she said maybe I ought to suck on a piece of ice anyway, in case my stomach needed settling. I really did feel okay, but to pacify Mama who liked to make over her baby, I went to the ice box and chipped off a small sliver of ice. It quickly melted in my mouth and I returned for a larger piece.

Mama said she'd better call Violet and tell her about Mr. Petty. She was still talking on the phone when I left. I had to go back to the corner to see what was happening.

They had found the body about noon, twenty minutes or so earlier, and already people were taking turns looking in the basement window. Evidently, Miss Louie Gladstone had been calling folks, like Mama and Aunt Violet said she always did the minute she heard somebody was dead. Both said they never could understand how Miss Louie never failed to know everything that happened before anybody else in town.

This was one time that she wasn't the first to know. There was no way Miss Louie could have known about Mr. Petty before I did. But however the news was being spread, it was spreading fast.

Suddenly it hit me that *The Reidsville Review* was bound to put out an extra. I jumped on my Rollfast bicycle and hurried down to the newspaper office. An hour and a half later I got one of the first bundles of extras hot off the press.

Within two hours after Smith Petty's body was found, *The Review* had 1,500 extras on the streets.

Joe Burton, who was in my grade at school and lived just a block away on Piedmont Street, showed up right behind me at the scene of the crime with his bundle of extras, both of us selling papers as fast as we could hand them out. What made it even better was that a lot of people were so excited and anxious to read all about it, that they would tell us to keep the change, if all they had was a dime.

I never saw so many people crowding into one small, treeless yard and spilling over into the street as I did that Saturday, September 3, 1927. By the middle of the afternoon, hundreds of Reidsville's and Rockingham County's curious — men, women and children (oddly more women than men) — had lined up and walked down the red clay slope to the basement where the badly decomposed body lay exposed in its shallow grave.

Louise Sharp would well remember that day, but not because she saw the body — she had no wish to see it. Louise, two years younger than her brother Tommy, my classmate at the Franklin Street Graded School, remembered something else: The awful odor that carried almost a quarter of a mile to the Sharp house, just beyond the S-curve where Lindsey Street straightened out and made a beeline to the West End.

After the shock of seeing the body dug up had about worn off, I went back for another, longer look. G. W. Windsor, a boyhood playmate, and I remember to this day Petty's B.V.D.s — the one-piece kind you stepped into - the dirty blanket, his body in a fetal position, knees drawn up to his chest.

Petty's bowed head was bashed-in and his matted hair looked longer than I remembered ever seeing it, making me wonder if maybe your hair really did keep growing after you were dead, like some people said.

Even after the coroner's inquest was concluded and the body removed to Wilkerson's Funeral Home, people continued to arrive late into the afternoon, queuing up to file by in fascination and gasp at the horror of what had so recently lain in the hole barely two feet deep with its lingering smell of death and decay that authenticated the macabre secret of the empty grave.

The discovery of the body in the basement was just the tip of the iceberg. Everybody else was just like Mama. What they wanted to know was how and why it got there.

2

S mith Petty was a man who moved around a lot. He was a cotton mill man and he went where the jobs were.

"That was the way it was in those days; you had to go where the work was," John Pettigrew, still sharp at almost ninety-two, recalled in May of 1991. "I remember working with Smith in Alabama when I was just a kid. He was right smart older than I was and he was an overseer. He had a temper, I can tell you that. But he wasn't a bad fellow, after you got to know him. I worked for him at Pomona Mill in Greensboro and Draper Mill in Leaksville. And we worked together at the mill here in town until I left to go to the cigarette factory.

"Smith was a good cotton mill man, but he was a heavy drinker. And sooner or later he'd pull a drunk and lay out. Liable to be out two weeks before he'd show up for work again. Far as I know, he did the same thing everywhere he ever worked. Sometimes he'd get back on and sometimes he wouldn't. I guess I'd have to say his drinking was the main reason he worked so many places. But that wasn't the only reason; sometimes the work would just run out and the mill would close."

Smith Thomas Petty, born in 1882 near Union, South Carolina, was the third of several children John Petty's first wife gave birth to before she died. Smith's father remarried and the babies kept coming until there were 12 children in all: four daughters and eight sons.

Working in cotton mills was all young Smith ever knew. But he couldn't stay put. He was in his early twenties when he found work in Virginia, where he fell in love with and married a dainty, soft-spoken young girl named Jeanne Bratton. Called Jennie by some, she was known to most as Janie Bratton.

The Bratton family had a good name and Janie's older brother Tom had been one of the men furnished a horse by the company to scour the countryside and recruit men and women to work in the new cotton mill built a few years after the turn of the century on the New River in the Virginia mountains by a Colonel Fries of Winston-Salem, North Carolina.

The village that sprang up around the mill was named Fries, pronounced "freeze," as was the colonel's name. Within a few years, many of its inhabitants would joke that the small Virginia town should be called "freeze" in winter and "fries" in summer.

Janie Bratton Petty was seventeen when her first child was born in Fries on August 30, 1906. She and Smith named their daughter Alma, and the proud papa would always grin when people remarked that his little girl sure did have his nose.

Smith Petty was thirty-eight years old and had worked in cotton mills in more different places than he cared to remember by the time he arrived in Reidsville with his wife and four children in 1920. The pleasant, slow-paced little town in north-central North Carolina was to be the end of the line for the wandering textile man, for in less than seven years he would be killed and hidden in a basement grave. And the aftermath that would follow the discovery of his decayed body would shock the quiet community as it had never been shocked before.

The Civil War had brought the railroad to Reidsville, and the railroad brought growth to the town that had been stagnating during the thirty years that followed its becoming a halfway station when the stage line was run from Danville, Virginia to Salisbury in the early 1830s. Located near the Virginia line, midway between Danville and Greensboro, the village had become, with the completion of the Piedmont Railroad in Reidsville in 1863, the principal station between the two cities. Within ten years, a hotel as well as a warehouse to sell leaf tobacco at auction had been built. During the next decade, four additional warehouses were built, with more planned.

Reidsville had been barely a village in the heart of a tobacco-growing region when William Lindsey began manufacturing plug tobacco in 1856. Most of the fifteen tobacco factories that had sprung up in the town by 1885 produced plug and twist tobacco, but two factories manufactured smoking tobacco and cigarettes.

By the turn of the century, many of the smaller tobacco businesses had faded away. But in 1911 something happened that would lead to Reidsville's developing into a major tobacco manufacturing center: The American Tobacco Company came to Reidsville and the F. R. Penn Tobacco Company, the biggest in town, became part of the American Tobacco Trust. But the tobacco monopoly created by Durham millionaire Buck Duke was dissolved that same year and the new operation became the F. R. Penn Branch, American Tobacco Company, with the founder's oldest son, Mr. Charlie Penn, at the helm. He soon became a vice president of the company with an office at its New York headquarters, but every weekend he took the train back to Reidsville to be with family and friends.

Mr. Charlie made a notable contribution to the company and to the town he so dearly loved when he perfected the blend for Lucky Strike cigarettes, which were first manufactured in 1916. The demand for the new cigarette continued to grow and within six years the local factory was "turning out a little better than one million Lucky Strike cigarettes each hour, and rounding out 10 hours every day in the week," according to an article in *The Reidsville Review* dated July 18, 1922.

The success of Lucky Strike cigarettes was undeniable proof that the Penn branch of the American Tobacco Company was indeed the economic heart of Reidsville.

Toward the end of the 1880s, some of the town's leading citizens had questioned the wisdom of placing such a heavy dependence on a single industry and decided economic diversification was needed. The textile industry seemed the obvious choice and by 1890 the Reidsville Cotton Mill was a reality. A community enterprise capitalized with $50,000 of common stock, the company was soon in financial difficulty. In 1892 it was reorganized as the Hermitage Cotton Mill, but in 1893 the business went into receivership under Colonel Henry Fries of Winston-Salem. Colonel Fries sold the mill to a group headed by Whitmell Stallings Forbes of Richmond, Virginia, who renamed it the Edna Cotton Mill for his oldest daughter. The presence of the mill created a nice blend of textiles and tobacco in the thriving little town of 8,000 people.

J. B. Pipkin, who would become president of Edna Mills Corporation in 1931, had been secretary-treasurer of the mill for twenty years when Smith Petty was hired in 1920 as an overseer earning what he described to his wife as a decent salary. An ordinary "doffer" in the cotton mill made only about half what the American Tobacco Company paid its cigarette "catchers," and many cotton mill families lived on the parents' combined income of under fifteen dollars a week in small, unpainted company houses on Paradise Alley, where here and there brave little rows of red geraniums sat in tin cans on tiny, rickety porches.

But the flowers were wasted on Smith Petty; all he saw was another narrow cotton mill street, just like all of them, ugly and depressing. He was glad he was making enough money to live somewhere else. For the time being, anyhow. His many disappointments and hard knocks had made a chronic worrier of Smith Petty and he had to struggle to keep from asking himself why his new job should last any longer than the others.

Alma Petty was fourteen; her sister, Thelma, was twelve; Woodrow was eight; and Smith, Jr. was two years old when the family moved into the old dormitory on Morehead Street, the first of several places they would live in Reidsville.

Jake Gardner lived with his parents in a small house on the south side of Morehead Street, between Main and Scales Streets, right across the street from the rambling old building called "The Dormitory." Originally the Rockingham Hotel, called a boarding house by some, it had been bought by Hugh Reid Scott, distinguished lawyer and legislator and grandson of Reidsville's founding father, Reuben Reid. Mr. Scott hired Mrs. C. J. Matthews as manager and used the building

Old Dormitory, first dwelling place of the Petty family in Reidsville. In foreground are, from left, Buck Link and cousins, Gladys Parrish Johnson and Ed Lewis.

as a dormitory for the women who came to town from their homes around the county to work in the cigarette factory, taking the men's places when they went off to war in 1917.

About all I can remember about the dormitory is a hazy impression of being in Jake Gardner's front yard and seeing people on the other side of the street sitting in rocking chairs on the long veranda that stretched across the front of the building. But Jake, five years older than I was, remembered when families lived in the dormitory, and he recalled that the Pettys lived in the western end of the structure, the part that was three stories high. Jake told me that he often saw Smith Petty sitting motionless in a porch rocker for what seemed an inordinately long time to a young boy. Always off to himself and always in the same position, Mr. Petty would sit with his elbows on his knees, hands clasped between his lower legs.

Perhaps he was worried about the future and brooding over the past, the jobs that had evaporated when mills closed, the jobs he couldn't hold because of his spree-drinking, the meanness that came out in him when he was full of liquor.

The Pettys never owned a home in Reidsville, and for whatever reasons, they seemed to move a lot. When they left the dormitory, they moved across the railroad, renting one of the eight apartments in the old building on Lawsonville Avenue that once housed a finishing

The Old Seminary, where the Pettys rented an apartment before moving to the house at the corner of Franklin and Lindsey Streets.

school for young ladies. Originally the Reidsville Female Seminary, the building was still called "the old seminary."

Diddle Hooper, whose family lived there when he was a child, remembered Smith Petty as a silent, solitary man he would occasionally see walking around in the yard. Recalling that Petty never spoke to him, Diddle said he figured it was because he was just a little kid.

But another explanation for Petty's moody reticence is more likely: He and the superintendent at the mill had trouble getting along, and that surely must have worried him, knowing that sooner or later he probably would be fired. Then it would be the same old story all over again: Hunting for a job in another town, getting hired, getting fired.

Past experience had taught Mrs. Petty that she couldn't depend on her husband's supporting the family, so early on she had found employment at Mrs. Cornie Irvin's ladies apparel store and stayed there until she went to work at Belk-Stevens the day the store opened on Tuesday, September 26, 1922.

Mrs. Petty, who had the piece goods department, never mixed with the younger clerks at the store and didn't like anybody to touch her fabrics unless they were buying. A meticulous woman, it was her habit after waiting on a customer to immediately return each bolt of cloth to its proper place in one of the neat stacks. Her penchant for neatness was also evident in her person. And sixty-five years later Frances Butler Royal, who was one of the younger clerks at Belk-Stevens when Mrs. Petty was there, would remember her as always "looking like she just jumped out of a bandbox."

Recognizing that every little bit helped, both the Petty girls had quit school in turn at sixteen to go to work. Alma had worked at a soda shop and sold tickets at the Grand Theatre before she was eventually hired as a dental assistant. After Alma had quit working at the picture show, her younger sister Thelma got her job selling tickets.

Mrs. Petty's niece, Annie Reedy, almost two years younger than Thelma, had come to live with them, and when Thelma wanted to have a night off, Annie Reedy would take Thelma's place at the box office.

Somewhere around the end of 1925 or early in January, 1926, the Pettys moved into the house on Lindsey Street. Smith Petty had lost his job several years earlier and had been working off and on in mills in other towns. In October, after Edna Cotton Mill had changed hands and his old nemesis was gone, Petty tried to get back on at the mill. But they had no work for him, so he began going out of town again, traveling from place to place in search of a job while his family remained at the Lindsey Street residence.

Whenever he had been lucky enough to find employment, it was Smith Petty's custom to write his father in South Carolina, but he had never bothered to let his wife know where he was. Then something would happen and he would lose out. And out of the blue, he would show up again. If he wasn't already drunk when he got home, he soon would be. Liquor made him mean, and the more he drank, the more he cursed and the more violent he became, giving his family good reason to be afraid of him.

Except for concluding that Smith Petty was a poor provider, the townspeople hadn't given much thought to his frequent absences. But when his brother had made the trip from Union, South Carolina, to attend Mrs. Petty's funeral in March and Smith Petty failed to show up, people began to wonder. Even if he was as sorry as some said, surely he would have come to his own wife's funeral. Unless he had met with foul play.

Mrs. Pearl Leath, Alma's Sunday school teacher, sent by Alma to fetch the Rev. H.B. Worley when Janie Petty was on her death bed. (Photo courtesy Laura Marie Dodson Johnston)

The Rev. H.B.Worley. (Photo courtesy Jo Abell Fahlstedt)

3

Janie Petty died at home on Wednesday night, March 9, 1927 at 11:30.

The next morning, Eugene Gatlin, who had been dating Alma since the previous summer, came by to see if there was anything he could do to help.

There certainly was, Alma said. Though still red-eyed from crying, she seemed to Gene to be bearing up well when she told him she needed to locate her father, so she could let him know the bad news. Gatlin dutifully went to the Western Union office and sent telegrams for Alma to Franklinton and Gastonia.

But the search for her father proved fruitless, and when Reverend W. B. Worley preached Mrs. Petty's funeral at 2:30 Friday afternoon at the Lindsey Street residence, Smith Petty was conspicuous by his absence.

All the employees of Belk-Stevens were able to attend the funeral in a body, since the store where Mrs. Petty had been employed for several years had closed for an hour out of respect for the deceased.

According to the *Reidsville Review*, "the floral tributes were large and beautiful, the room in which the casket rested being almost banked with flowers, and the grave literally covered."

The gossip had started before Mrs. Petty's body was cold and by the time the burial was over and the mourners had left Greenview Cemetery, it was hard to find anybody who hadn't already heard what was being repeated for the truth: Double pneumonia might have been what carried her away, like the doctor said; but something else was what really killed her. And she was only thirty-eight years old.

Always a strong-willed girl, Alma had surprised her family a few years earlier with her sensitivity when she began writing sentimental poems about mother love, as well as other subjects common to budding poets.

Alma loved her mother, but it was her daddy that Alma had been so crazy about when she and Blanche Moore were good friends and often walked to school together. Blanche would recall sixty-eight years later that Smith Petty often used to play cards with Alma, Thelma and her when the Pettys lived in the old seminary. When asked if Mrs. Petty ever joined them, Blanche shook her head an emphatic no, adding that they never saw her; she always kept to herself in another room.

On July 7, 1927, four months after her mother's death, Alma, not quite twenty-one, married Eugene S. Gatlin, who was ten years her senior.

Gatlin, who had come to Reidsville several years earlier to take a job as the movie projectionist at the Grand Theatre, hadn't been in town long before he realized that he missed the fellowship of the Lowell Masonic Lodge where he had been a member, and he had his membership transferred to the Reidsville Lodge, effective August 1, 1924. He soon became a volunteer fireman, and when offered the position of chief, he gave up his job at the picture show and went to work full-time for the fire department.

The firehouse, on the southwest corner of Morehead and Market Streets, was only a couple of minutes away from Gardner Drug Company on South Scales Street, where nine or ten times a day the restless chief habitually dropped in, drinking at least two Coca Colas on each visit to the soda fountain. Sometimes he might drink as many as three or four, one right behind the other, and be back in an hour for more. Drugstore employee James Thompson, who for some time had been watching Gatlin with growing fascination, decided one hot summer day when business was slow that he would surreptitiously keep count, just for fun. The total so surprised James that sixty-five years later he would emphasize that he had double-checked his count to be sure it was correct, for at the end of that long ago day when he had tallied up his pencil marks, the total number of six-ounce glasses of Coca Cola quaffed by the fire chief was an incredible twenty-eight! Likely, it was a record for Gene and surely one never equaled since.

Alma was remembered sixty-five years later by Virginia Meador Roberts as a friendly young woman with a sweet personality who worked as a dental assistant and receptionist for her father, Dr. J.

Gene Gatlin, second from right, wearing cap, behind the soda fountain at drugstore operated by H.E. Link, who became foreman of the Grand Jury that indicted Alma.

Gene Gatlin, left, with firemen Tom Dallas and Frank Trent, right, before he became chief.
(Photo courtesy Reidsville Fire Department)

R. Meador. Virginia was nine or ten years old when she dropped by her father's office on the second floor of the Citizens Bank building on the southwest corner of Gilmer and Scales Streets and was invited by Alma, who was not yet married and still lived on Lindsey Street, to come visit her, reminding the child that she didn't live far from Virginia's house on Maple Avenue. They would make homemade candy, she promised. She knew Dr. Meador wouldn't let his wife make candy at home because he said it would rot the children's teeth. The secret shared that day between the little girl and Alma became one of Virginia's fondest memories.

Alma was remembered by Cecilia Scott Hester as an exceptionally good basketball player, while Charlie Fowlkes remembered Alma's sister, Thelma, as the best dancer he ever saw. Classmates and acquaintances I talked to recalled various things about the two sisters, but all agreed that they were as different as night and day and didn't look like sisters at all.

One man recalled that Alma had "a cute pug nose." And like her younger brother, Woodrow, Alma did indeed have her father's retrousse nose. Thelma and Smith, Jr., the youngest child, had their mother's straight, rather patrician nose.

Alma, who was about five-feet-four, was remembered by one old acquaintance as having a somewhat husky build, a description that prompted another person to say maybe so but he wouldn't call her a large person. There was general agreement, though, among the people I spoke with that Alma was heavier through the shoulders than most females her height and her hips were perhaps a little broader than average. Thelma, with a slim figure and pretty legs, was petite like her mother. And Mildred Waynick said she would never forget Thelma's china doll skin, so pretty and smooth she didn't need any makeup.

Pitt Wilkerson remembers Thelma's taking classmates on joy rides in Charlie Barnett's Buick after school. Charlie was older than Thelma and already working as an automobile mechanic when the object of his affections was in the eighth grade. As had been the case with Alma, Thelma was older than most of her classmates, probably because of their father's habit of moving his family from town to town before they settled in Reidsville.

Far from an Adonis, Charlie Barnett had the added disadvantage of speaking with a high-pitched nasal whine, and the only way he knew to try and "make time" with the beautiful Thelma was to let her drive his car. According to her friends, Thelma never cared anything about Charlie, but she did enjoy driving his Buick anytime she wanted to. Turner Watlington told me about riding his bicycle to see Thelma when he was "trying to court her," and she would take him for a spin in Charlie's Buick. She was to put the car to more constructive use at a later date when she drove her younger brother, Smith, Jr., to Oxford Orphanage, where he would be admitted on March 26, 1928, a few months before his tenth birthday.

Nobel King, a classmate of Alma's, remembered her love of rambunctious fun. Almost seventy years later, King would recall the time Alma and Reda Roman brought stink bombs into the classroom after big recess and, with tomboyish daring, rolled them down the aisles where Horace Burton and several other boys reached their legs out from their desks and stomped them to release the sulfur fumes.

In spite of her mischievousness, or perhaps because the other kids secretly admired Alma's boldness, she was elected secretary of her eighth grade class. Mutt Burton, whose desk was across the aisle from Alma's, thought she was pretty. And the inset photograph of her in the 1923 yearbook, *The Souvenir*, pictures her as an attractive young lady, although she delighted in doing such unladylike things as "bumping."

Bumping was done by two people each holding an arm and a leg of a third person, who was swung back and forth a few times before bumping another person positioned to receive the blow by bending over from the waist. Hard butt-to-butt contact was made, which frequently knocked the accommodating target person, sturdy or not, off balance.

Alma once used a different and far rougher version of bumping, and when found out, she was punished by being sent home from school. Angry at a girl for tattling on a classmate, Alma had decided to teach her a lesson. After allegedly bullying another girl into helping her, the two swung the tattler into one of the big oak trees on the schoolground. The victim of the bumping was too sore to make it to school the next day and missed several more days before she was able to return to her classes.

Alma was remembered by eighth grade classmates for different things, but references to her quick temper was a constant that recurred with prophetic frequency. One woman remembered her as a domineering sixteen-year-old and said if she wasn't sneering, she often had a "foolish grin" on her face. Whatever Alma's expression, you had better not cross her, the woman said, since to do so would result in her "exploding like a firecracker." A male classmate agreed that Alma had a temper but wanted it known that she was all right as long you didn't make her mad. If you made her mad, she would lay a real cussing on you, the man said, stressing that the profanities Alma used were those more commonly spouted by men.

While conceding that Alma was two or three years older than most of her classmates in the eighth grade, one of the girls who was in Alma's room at Franklin Street Graded School told me that Alma was already doing things that the parents of most of the other girls wouldn't allow them to do until they were in the eleventh grade. That was their senior year back then.

It seems likely that rather than Alma's being allowed to do what she wanted to, she simply went ahead and did as she liked without worrying about it. Parental supervision must have been minimal, especially for the oldest child, since Alma's father was rarely home and Mrs. Petty had her hands full trying to take care of her family. Working as a clerk six days a week must have kept Mrs. Petty worn out and she surely longed for more time at home so she could be the mother she wanted to be.

As bored with the immaturity of her classmates as she was with school, Alma knew exactly what she was doing the day she sealed her fate as a schoolgirl by "talking back to the teacher." When Miss Donie Counts, the English teacher, asked why she hadn't gotten her lessons, Alma's sassy response was that she'd had more important things to do than study her lessons.

Some think Alma was expelled, while others say she quit school to go to work. But for whatever reason, she left school for good when she was sixteen.

Although the whole town was shocked, nobody was more surprised than Gene Gatlin when his wife of two months was arrested less than twenty minutes after the body of her father was discovered in its shallow grave under a coal pile in the basement.

The thirty-year-old fire chief's surprise was compounded when he was picked up as well and brought to city hall, where he was placed in the custody of local officers and held for questioning. However, he was released that afternoon after the authorities were convinced that he was not involved.

Alma Gatlin was not so fortunate. Arrested at the dental office of Dr.J. R. Meador, she still wore her white uniform when she was taken by Sheriff Chunk Smith and his deputies to the municipal building, where she was searched by Lola Young, who worked for the city, and Mary Stokes Dailey, a secretary for the law firm of Glidewell, Dunn and Gwyn, whose offices were located in the building. Later, Mary would tell a friend that she was scared to death that Alma might have a pistol in her purse.

But Mary needn't have worried. There was no desperation in Alma's demeanor. She remained as calm as she had been at the dentist's office when the sheriff had said to her, "It is a very disagreeable duty I have, but I must arrest you on a murder warrant." Alma had shown no emotion when she answered that she was ready to go, and she seemed not at all concerned when she was brought to city hall and searched before the coroner's hearing began.

Alma's expression was a picture of composure when she was charged with the murder of her father and taken to the county jail at Wentworth.

Rockingham County Sheriff J.F. "Chunk" Smith. (Photo courtesy N.C. Collection, UNC Library at Chapel Hill)

Alma Petty Gatlin outside Rockingham County
Courthouse at Wentworth during her trial. (Photo
courtesy N.C. Collection, UNC Library at Chapel Hill)

4

"Pretty Mrs. Alma Petty Gatlin" was the way the accused murderess was described in *The Reidsville Review's* extras on the Saturday she was arrested, and Alma asked the bespectacled jailer John W. Irving, affectionately called Uncle Johnny by some, to register her as *The Review* had it. The fifty-five-year-old man, who enjoyed smoking an underslung pipe filled with his favorite Prince Albert tobacco, probably found Alma pretty. Indeed, it would have been unusual had he not found personable the mature woman who had outgrown her schoolgirl tomboyishness.

Everybody seemed to like Alma and there was no reason for Irving to be the exception. Still, that didn't mean that the idea to allow his star prisoner to have all the comforts of home had originated with him; though the sisterhood of gossips never doubted for one minute that it was the jailer's doing. Clucking their disapproval, the gossips could not imagine that anybody would think otherwise. Actually, it was Alma's lawyers who had set the machinery in motion by referring to the sheriff her request that she be allowed to brighten up her quarters. Visualizing the great improvement over the graffiti that prisoners traditionally scribbled on the drab gray walls, Sheriff Chunk Smith, the jailer's boss, surely approved with alacrity.

Soon lace curtains hung on the windows with chintz draperies to match the cover on the couch in her well-ventilated cell on the second floor of the jail. Alma painted the walls herself, tinting them a light green, and decided to paint the bars as well while she was at it.

Other homelike touches appeared when Alma hung on the wall two pictures of her mother: one was a photograph of the dead woman

Rockingham County Jailer John W. Irving and his wife. (Photo courtesy Francis Anderson Family Collection)

in her coffin, surrounded by funereal flowers; the other, a life-sized photograph, hand-tinted in pinks and cream, dwarfed the picture of Alma's husband Eugene Gatlin, which sat on the box she used for a dresser. In the coming months, increasing numbers of pictures of movie stars, cut out of magazines, would plaster the cell walls.

In typical small town fashion, the gossips accused the jailer of playing favorites, even though all Irving had done was follow orders. And of course, it was inevitable that some wag would say if Uncle Johnny had judged the contest sponsored by Reidsville merchants fifteen months earlier when Alma was nineteen, she would have won first place instead of coming in second behind Elsie Benson.

Both girls won train trips to California; and one of the losers, envious of Alma's second prize trip, was quick to point out that it wasn't really a popularity contest, as many called it; all you had to do to win was to sell the most votes, and selling votes and being popular were two different things. Still, the losing contestant's cynicism didn't change the fact that Alma was indeed a popular and outgoing girl. She was not however a "beauty contest winner," as newspapers seeking to sensationalize their stories would claim.

Late Sunday afternoon, when Alma received a reporter from *The Reidsville Review* and a correspondent from *The Charlotte Observer*, she greeted them cordially with the gentility of a hostess inviting guests into her parlor. She was wearing a silken dressing robe and reclining on her cot when the reporters entered her cell; but she immediately tucked her bare feet under her robe, sat up, smiled warmly and asked if the town had quieted down any. They could hardly have failed to consider her question a strange one to ask on the day of her murdered father's funeral, but their response was simply that Reidsville was reasonably calm. She answered that they'd had right much excitement over there for the last day or two. Since the newspapermen had agreed not to question Mrs. Gatlin, she was asked only if she would like to make a formal statement. She laughed and said not now but maybe later. Then she solemnly added that the other side was doing all the talking now and everything was against her. If she decided to do some talking, she would let them know.

Depending on circumstances, the kindly jailer could be adamant in his determination not to let the press bother his prisoner, the "girl-bride," as one newspaper described her, even though she had turned twenty-one about two months after she married Eugene Gatlin.

The NO VISITORS ALLOWED sign on the sheet of yellow paper which had been hung on the barred door meant exactly what it said, as far as John Irving was concerned. However, on one occasion he did explain to persistent reporters that she'd already been bothered enough, having been in consultation with her lawyers all day.

Rockingham County Jail at Wentworth, where Alma was imprisoned for almost six months before her trial. (Photo courtesy N.C. Collection, UNC Library at Chapel Hill)

In her article, which appeared Monday evening, September 5, 1927 in the *Greensboro Daily Record,* Staff Correspondent Nell Craig, obviously impressed with Alma, wrote that "prior to the appearance of the jailer, Mrs. Gatlin had shown a friendliness when she peered eagerly through the bars from her second story cell, her pretty face framed by her black bobbed hair, and answered the query as to where the jailer could be found with the ready reply, 'I think you'll find him at the door down there.' She possesses an unusually attractive speaking voice, which has peculiarly rich contralto tones. Her manner indicated a freedom from care."

As people still do today in smaller towns and communities, most in Reidsville knew everybody else in 1927. Even if they didn't know them personally, they usually knew who they were. So when the fire chief's new wife was arrested and charged with the murder of her father the local citizens just did not know what to think. Alma had always made friends easily and was so well thought of, nobody could understand how she could have done what she was accused of doing. But these same people had to admit that they found it just as hard to believe that a preacher would make up the story of Alma's alleged confession. And more and more developments were coming to light that seemed to substantiate the validity of what Rev. Pardue insisted Alma had confessed to him: that she had killed her father.

Alma stuck to her story that she had made no such confession and according to the jailer, she would never show any serious signs of being worried during the more than five months she was to lounge in her cell in the county jail awaiting trial. Perhaps her lawyers had Alma convinced that they would be able to get her off.

On the afternoon of the day the body was found, an inquest had been called by Dr. Charles R. Wharton, the county coroner. Dr. S. G. Jett, who had made the initial examination of the grisly remains, testified that he found "a wound on the right side of the head five inches long, which fractured the skull, and also another wound over the left eye sufficient to cause a fracture of the skull, thought sufficient to cause almost instant death." The testimony of Dr. M. P. Cummings was basically the same.

Dr. Wharton's duty to establish the cause of death was done; "the courts would have to delve more deeply into the evidential aspects of the case," as he explained to P. T. Stiers, Alma's attorney, who wanted to question Rev. Pardue.

Evangelist "Thunderbolt Tom" Pardue, who told authorities Alma confessed to him of murdering her father. (Photo courtesy of Mrs. Hilda Pardue)

Former Chief of Police Charles W. Jackson, who knew Smith Petty well, was the first witness at the inquest. He testified that the body, found two feet under the ground, was indeed Petty. Elmo Moricle, Mrs. John Price, Johnny McAdams, W. S. Black and W. J. Black, all acquaintances of Petty, also testified that they had identified the body. It was Smith Petty's strong, thick neck, they agreed, his teeth and his general build that made them sure it was Petty.

During the coroner's hearing, Alma Petty Gatlin had seemed not at all perturbed. Immaculate in her white uniform, she primped her hair while looking around with interest and showed no dismay when Rev. Thomas Pardue told the jury of her confession of murder, allegedly made to him in May.

Alma did not take the stand, but P. T. Stiers took advantage of the pause in the proceedings, while the coroner's jury was out deliberating, to tell a newspaperman that Alma would never be convicted, that she was guiltless. Asked what the defense would be, he smiled knowingly and said it was too early to lay all his cards on the table. When the reporter persisted and asked the attorney if his client would seek to show that another committed the crime in her presence or that it was a self-defense case, his only answer was a sly smile. Then the soft-spoken lawyer said earnestly, "This woman has made no effort to escape. She has been here regularly since December. She could have run away long ago. It is impossible that she can be guilty of murder and betray not the slightest indication of fear or of a troubled mind."

Earlier that Saturday afternoon, Scott Fillman, an officer of the First National Bank, had just stepped out the door of the bank when he was recruited by one of the deputies rounding up people downtown to serve on the coroner's jury.

The banker was made its foreman, and when the coroner's jury had concluded their deliberations and returned to the room where the hearing was being held, Fillman had this to say: "After viewing the body identified as the body of Smith T. Petty and having heard the evidence offered, we find on the evidence offered that Smith T. Petty came to his death at the hands of his daughter Alma Petty, now Mrs. Eugene Gatlin, by blows administered by some heavy instrument. After hearing the evidence, we recommend that Alma Petty Gatlin be taken into custody by the sheriff of Rockingham County."

As she was being led to jail, when Rev. Pardue tried to explain to her the reasons for his action, Alma had looked him squarely in the eye, smiled, and said it was "all right."

5

Alma Petty was nineteen the first time she heard the Reverend Thunderbolt Tom Pardue preach. The dynamic evangelist was holding a revival in a tent on the southeast corner of Main and Settle Streets, and the old-time religion he espoused and his dramatic delivery had affected her deeply.

Soon after the preacher concluded his local revival and moved on to preach on sin and redemption in other towns, an evangelistic club had been formed, and Alma, who was an active member of the Church of Christ on North Scales Street, became an enthusiastic member of the club. An ardent admirer of the man and his message, Alma was excited when Rev. Pardue agreed to come back to Reidsville the following year.

Encouraged by the warm reception he had received, it occurred to the preacher that the friendly little town could well be the place where his longtime dream of one day having his own church might be realized. So in the spring of 1927, he moved with his family from Winston-Salem to make Reidsville the home base for his evangelistic ministry.

Sixty-five years later, William Oakley, a neighbor and boyhood friend of the preacher's son, would recall how hard Rev. Thomas F. Pardue worked for the privilege of doing the Lord's work, even selling silverware at revival meetings to keep going. Many times William would see the preacher coming home, after conducting a revival out of town, with his Chrysler loaded with vegetables and fruits, and sometimes live chickens. In those days of tight money, it was not unusual for many people to pay preachers and doctors with what they raised.

. . .

It seemed a prophetic beginning when the preacher didn't have to use his dilapidated tent and opened his 1927 revival in what he called a tabernacle. But it was really only Pinnix's Warehouse, changed around until fall of the year, when it would again be put to the use for which it had been built. Then, through the dust and autumn heat would come the sound of the auctioneer's fast chant — selling tobacco, pile after pile; row after row of the "golden weed." That was what a lot of folks liked to call the cured tobacco that was manufactured into Lucky Strike cigarettes in the Reidsville plant of The American Tobacco Company, which everybody called "the factory."

Tobacco was cultivated in fields all over Rockingham County, with mud-chinked log barns standing sentinel. When the tobacco was ripe, farmers would cut the stalks bearing the broad green leaves down the middle, leaving the split stalks joined at the top so they could be slung in rows over tobacco sticks and hung in barns to be flue-cured to a rich, bright yellow. It took two barns to make an average load of 1500 pounds of cured tobacco, which was covered with quilts and hauled into town, usually in horse-drawn wagons, by farmers hoping to get a good price for their only cash crop. If a farmer thought his tobacco sold too low, he wouldn't let it go; he'd "take it in," as they said, and then see Mr. Crutch, whose full name was G. E. Crutchfield. He lived next door to the Links and was a buyer for The American Tobacco Company. All the children liked him and so did everybody else. Especially the farmers. You couldn't find a farmer who wouldn't tell you the same thing: If need be, Mr. Crutch would always see to it that their tobacco brought what it was worth.

For Rev. Pardue's revival, a crude platform had been put up at one end of the warehouse. On the platform stood a pulpit, behind which sat several rows of chairs grouped together to form the choir loft. Facing the platform were what looked like enough seats for half of Reidsville; long benches made of lumber so rough Mama joked it was a wonder somebody didn't stick a splinter in their behind. Especially if they were wearing a flimsy dress, like the flappers were fond of wearing. Of course, if they were real flappers, they weren't very likely to be going to the revival. If what folks said was right, a real flapper would probably rather be off in some roadhouse smoking cigarettes and doing the Charleston. And maybe proving how modern she was by turning up a silver hip flask and taking a big swig of her boyfriend's bootleg whiskey.

Alma Petty was said to like to have a good time, but I wouldn't have called her a flapper type, even though she did have bobbed hair. She wasn't anything like I imagined the flapper looked with the "turned-up nose and rolled-down hose" in the song my brother Buck used to sing and play on the ukulele.

The previous year, when Rev. Pardue had been conducting a revival in Reidsville, he had come to know Alma as a zealous nineteen-year-old who was active in religious work.

She didn't disappoint the preacher and was present almost every night at the services he was holding at the tobacco warehouse in the spring of 1927. A few nights after Mother's Day, Alma waited until the rest of the congregation was gone and asked the preacher to go into the choir loft with her. He assured her that anything she told him would be confidential, never dreaming of the enormity of the confession Alma would make.

6

After Alma's confession to Rev. Pardue of the terrible thing she had done, the evangelist had endured two days of agonized searching of his Missionary Baptist soul, and he prayed long and hard for divine guidance before going to the local authorities. His conscience simply would not allow him to keep the awful secret any longer.

He knew there were people in Reidsville who regarded him as nothing more than a jackleg preacher, but whatever they might think of him was no reason for the sheriff's office and the police department to be dragging their feet; and the distraught evangelist resented the implication that they didn't believe him. An insulting way to treat a man of God who was trying to do his civic duty. He certainly would never have made up such a tale.

He had lost ten pounds in a week. He couldn't eat, couldn't sleep, and he was in the midst of his revival meeting.

On May 20, the evangelist's dream of one day getting his own church had begun to materialize with the organization of the Lawsonville Avenue Baptist Church and the promise of a new house of worship to be completed by October. Rev. Pardue praised the Lord and joyfully thanked Him for answering his prayers. But what should have been the happiest day of his life was marred by frustration. Nothing was being done about Alma's confession.

Since the Reidsville authorities wouldn't give him any satisfaction, Rev. Pardue decided to take matters into his own hands. He intended to protect his reputation as a minister and dedicated servant of the Lord by proving that he was no liar, and, in the process, he meant to see justice done. So on June 10, 1927, he went to the Home Detective Agency in Greensboro and related the story of the alleged confession to Charles W. Noell, a former police officer turned detective. Noell was to have trouble with the law himself before the end of the year, when he allegedly intimidated and attempted to bribe a state's witness in another case. Whether he ever stood trial is not known.

On the following day, Pardue had accompanied the detective to the house at 78 Lindsey Street, where the decomposed body of Smith T. Petty would be discovered in less than three months. Mr. and Mrs. John Price had moved into the gray cottage on March 23, after Alma and the rest of her family moved into an apartment in the Gant house on the southwest corner of Lawsonville Avenue and McCoy Street just two weeks after the death of Janie Petty on March 9.

When Detective Noell went to the former Petty residence on Lindsey Street, he talked with the new tenants and requested that they not permit anyone to visit the basement without official authority. This upset Mrs. Price, who worked in the office at the cotton mill where Smith Petty had been employed as an overseer until about four years earlier, when he lost out with a change of superintendents. After that, he had found work in mills in other towns. Even members of his family wouldn't know where he was for months and months at a time; then he would reappear for a few weeks of drinking and being mean to his family, as Alma was later to describe to Solicitor Gwyn her father's short and infrequent visits home.

Smith Petty always followed the same pattern: Just as suddenly as he had arrived, he would be gone again. But this last absence was the longest ever, and rumors were rampant that he had met with foul play and that his daughter Alma was involved. No wonder Mrs. Price, her nerves already frayed almost to the breaking point, had been so rattled by Detective Noell's intimation of what they might find in her basement.

Alma, a friend of Mrs. Price's younger sister, Blanche Moore, sometimes visited Blanche in the family home, where Mrs. Price and her husband had lived with her parents until the couple moved to the Lindsey Street house. Knowing Alma and her daddy as well as she did and speculating on how true the rumors were was upsetting enough to Mrs. Price, but when Pardue had brought the detective to her house and he warned her about the basement, it was almost more than she could take. She had tried not to think about it, but she couldn't help herself. The thought of what might be buried in the basement had made her blood run cold that warm June day in 1927.

7

After Pardue and the detective left the Lindsey Street cottage, they went to City Attorney D. F. Mayberry's office, where Detective Noell offered to find the body and clear up the case for three hundred dollars. Mayberry talked with City Manager Joe Womack, whose answer was the city would handle the affair themselves.

That put the preacher right back where he had started. When he had gone to the police with the story of Alma's confession of the murder of her father, he felt that he might as well have been telling them about a hallucination for all the credence they seemed to place in his story.

He had done just about everything he could think of, including communicating with Governor Angus W. McLean. He had gone to see Solicitor Porter Graves, whom he had known in Winston-Salem, and was told that the Reidsville authorities would have to handle the case. The preacher thanked him for his time without bothering to tell him that he had already been to them and had been given the impression that they thought he was just a crackpot evangelist trying to get his name in the paper with a wild story of murder.

When Pardue had accused the city administration of being derelict in their duty, a joint statement was issued from Sheriff J. F. Smith and Solicitor Allen H. Gwyn saying they believed there was no dereliction of duty on the part of town officers. When they had told Pardue they "could do nothing," they were all working quietly to one end: to solve the murder. It was not because they refused to act.

Still upset, the preacher didn't believe them at first, but he changed his mind after he cooled down and reminded himself of how he really felt about the solicitor. Rev. Pardue firmly believed him to be a fair and conscientious man who would not compromise his integrity and be a party to issuing a statement that was not true. If he could get Gwyn to agree to sit down with him and let him tell the full story, the preacher was convinced the solicitor would take the necessary steps to speed things up.

On August 22, Rev. Pardue took his story to Gwyn. The evangelist told the solicitor basically the same story he later told two Greensboro reporters who interviewed him at his home. Told in Rev. Pardue's own words, the story, which appeared in the *Greensboro Daily Record*, follows: "About three months ago, I was holding a series of revival meetings in a local tobacco warehouse. Miss Alma attended the services often. One night, about three weeks after the opening of the meeting, she came to the altar under a deep conviction.

"Two nights later, she came again, and I saw that she could not get a victory. I have been in this work for fifteen years, and when anyone remains troubled like that and cannot get peace, especially after the deep conviction that she had had, I know that there is some sin troubling them. I asked her to tell me what it was. A few nights later, she came to the altar again, and this time, too, she lingered, unable to gain a victory. After the others had left, she asked me to go into the choir loft with her. I had told her that I would keep secret anything she had to say, but when I made that promise I never dreamed of the horrible story she had to tell. I thought it was some minor offense, over which she was troubling herself.

"She sobbed out that she had committed two of the biggest sins in the world, and asked me if I thought she could get forgiveness. I told her there was forgiveness for any sin, except blasphemy against the Holy Spirit, and that I was certain she had not committed this offense. She told me that she had killed her father. I was horrified, and could not listen to the story then. I have never been so amazed, for I have known her for a year. A year before, I had conducted a revival here, and she had been a member of the evangelistic club that was formed afterward. She had been active in religious work.

"A few days later she came to my house and told the whole story. I said to her, 'Alma, my heart is with you and I want you to tell me what is on your mind and (in your) heart.'

"She told me that three years ago there was some family disagreement, the nature of which I do not know. Anyway, her father whipped her, and she swore at the time that she would kill him. She got a pistol and for two years, she told me, she carried it, seeking an opportunity to kill her father. She never got the chance, though, to do it without being found out. Then she attended the revival services a year ago, and put away the gun. She had also tried to poison him a number of times, she said.

"Sometime around Christmas, she went home one Sunday evening and found her father choking her mother, she said. She grabbed hold of him, and for some time had the advantage of him, pressing his back against the bureau. Then, he gained the mastery, and gave her a whipping.

"'I swore then that I would kill him before morning,' she told me. 'He did everything he could to annoy us that night. He played the talking machine and sang and cursed until after midnight.'

"I asked her if he was drinking, and she said no. 'Late that night he went down in the cellar and beat on the floor with the ax to bother them,' she said. 'Sometime later he went to bed.'

"'The next morning I got up at five o'clock and went down into the cellar in my pajamas to get the ax,' she told me. 'I knew it was there, because I had heard him beating on the floor with it the night before. I brought it upstairs and started to kill him while he slept, but I thought if I killed him in bed, the others would find it out. So I decided to wait until after my mother and sister had gone to work and kill him at breakfast. They went to work about 7:30. I placed the ax behind the kitchen door, so he wouldn't see it, and I called him to breakfast. He came in and washed his face and hands. I had placed his plate so that his back would be to the kitchen door. While he was eating his cereal, I put the ax beside the door facing, and was frying him an egg.'

"She told me that while he was eating the egg, she came in with the ax to kill him while she had the drop on him. I asked her which edge she struck him with, and she said with the blunt edge.

"'I raised the ax up in both hands with all my strength, and struck him on the head,' she said. 'The blood was awful. It streamed all over the place; all over him, on me, over the wall and down on his egg plate. His head fell over in the plate, and I stood there thinking to myself, now I have killed him!'

"He lay there for about two minutes, she said, and then suddenly rolled over in the floor. He opened his eyes and looked at her, saying, 'Alma, why are you trying to kill me?'

"It took him an hour and forty-five minutes to die, she told

47

me. He talked to her off and on. I asked her what he said.

"'He had always said he didn't believe in Hell,' she said, 'so I asked him, now, do you believe in Hell?' and he said, 'Yes, and I want you to pray for me, Alma, for I am going to die. You have killed me.'

"'Did you pray for him?' I asked her.

"'No,' she answered me, and she smiled when she said it.

"'I said to him,' she told me, 'Papa, ever since I swore to kill you three years ago, I have said that if I ever saw you dying I would spit in your face, but under the circumstances I won't do that.'

"I asked her if she cried while he was dying, and she said no.

"He started groaning, she said, and she was afraid the neighbors would hear, so she put her hand over his mouth. He bit her fingernail off and scratched her hand, she said, and for several days she had to wear a bandage.

"And after a while, he got stronger, and got a hold on the ax. She saw that she would have to do something to break his hold, she said. She thought about the galvanized pipe which connected the water pipes with the range in the kitchen, so she dragged him in there, and finished him off with two blows on the head.

"'Then,' she continued in her story to me, 'I knew that I would have to be quick, for he would soon get stiff, so in a hurry I took off his top clothes and mine off and burned them. Then I wrapped him in blankets and put his body in a trunk, which I put in a closet in the front room. I certainly had to work hard to get all that blood cleaned up before the others came home. My hair was covered with blood, too, until I looked like a stuck hog.'

"'Alma,' I said, 'you know you didn't get it all cleaned up. The others must have seen it and asked questions.'

"'No, they didn't,' she said, 'I cleaned it every bit up.'

"'The second day after that, blood began to run down out of the trunk and drip through the closet floor into the cellar,' she said. 'He began to smell terribly - and if you go down there right now you can still smell a bad odor in that closet.

"'A Dodge sedan drove up and took the body away. I dug the grave myself and did all the work. Nobody helped me, and nobody knew about it.'

"I told her that the only thing for her to do was to tell the police all about it. I realized that it was her soul that I was dealing with. She said, 'Never. I'll die and go to Hell before I'll tell them about it. And if you tell them I'll deny telling you anything about it. I'll die on the witness stand swearing it is a lie.'

"I said, 'Alma, you know you didn't do all that by yourself. Someone helped you to get the body away. You don't know how to drive a car and you couldn't have loaded the body.' She repeated that no one helped her, and would not explain about the body.

"'Alma,' I said to her, 'try to put yourself in my place. Murder will out. This thing will be found out sooner or later. You can't keep it concealed, even if I keep quiet. When it is discovered, and you are placed on the witness stand, your lawyer will ask you why didn't you tell someone about this? As an intelligent young woman, you will answer, I did; I told the preacher. Then, I will be condemned for keeping silent. People will ask what kind of preacher is this that conceals a terrible crime like that?'

"'But in no way could I prevail on her to confess to the officers.

"'I didn't see her anymore after that until in June, when I met her at a soda fountain here. She stated that she had been busy in religious work, and that she had led public prayer for the first time just a few days before. She also admitted that she had been drunk once since she had made the confession. I have heard it said about town that she went to Greensboro with some friends the night after she made the confession to me, got drunk, and had to pay a $50 fine to get out of it.

"'She never told me what the other sin to which she had referred was.'"

Even though Solicitor Gwyn's earlier idea had been to conduct an investigation that would prove there had been no murder, he wanted to be fair to the preacher, so he had agreed to see him at his office and hear him out. He listened carefully to every detail as the preacher told his story and believed him when he declared that it was a matter of conscience with him and he could not keep secret Alma's confession that she had murdered her father.

The solicitor was further convinced of Rev. Pardue's sincerity when he said he realized that his reputation as a man and a preacher was at stake when he revealed a penitent's confession, but he was compelled to do what he felt was the right thing, both as a citizen and a minister of the gospel.

Feeling certain that Rev. Pardue had told him the story of Alma's confession as honestly and as accurately as he could reconstruct it, Solicitor Gwyn decided that a hearing was in order.

8

What earlier had been a somewhat casual investigation was given impetus by the arrival in Reidsville of two detectives sent by Governor Angus McLean, who had been contacted by Solicitor Gwyn. The solicitor and the sheriff had joined forces in an accelerated search for Smith Petty's body; and on several occasions the young solicitor had jumped into his car, rushed to a rural wooded spot to investigate the report of a suspicious fresh mound of dirt, rolled up his sleeves and started digging, only to find another dog's grave.

Recognizing the pressing need for solid leads, Gwyn had instigated a hearing, which was held on Wednesday, August 31, 1927. However, he told newsmen who called the next day that he was not in a position to discuss the case. He saw no need to tell them that he, Sheriff J. F. Smith, and Police Chief Allie Pettigrew had all been working on the case since August 19, but when questioned further he consented to certain answers. He said the hearing was "for the purpose of ascertaining the whereabouts and status of Smith Petty, who has been missing for several months." He said that no arrests had been made, and he took pains to describe the hearing as more an investigation than the bringing of definite charges against any person. That was all he could tell them, he said, since he was not yet certain what other steps would be taken.

One reporter, anxious to sniff out some special news, had gone to the solicitor's office and was told by his secretary that "Mr. Gwyn was not talking to newspapermen at that stage of the game." Determined to get something out of his visit, he reported to his paper that "to those who have frequented courts, it was easy to see that the young woman was doing nothing other than typing evidence. The reportorial assumption is that it was the testimony given during Wednesday's hearing." His guess was undoubtedly right, and sixty-four years later, I had the good fortune to obtain a copy of that transcript.

To preserve the authenticity of the transcript, which appears below, I did not correct misspellings and errors in punctuation. However, to protect privacy, I changed a few names (indicated by asterisks).

STATE OF NORTH CAROLINA
COUNTY OF ROCKINGHAM

The purpose of this meeting held in the office of Glidewell, Dunn & Gwyn, Reidsville, N. C. is to inquire into the state and condition of Mr. Smith Petty. The following witnesses have been called for the purpose of this inquiry: Mrs. Alma Petty Gatlin, Sheriff J. F. Smith, Rev. Pardue, Joe Womack (city manager), R. A. Stokes (deputy sheriff), Eugene Gatlin, Blanche Moore, Mrs. John Price, Janie Winkler*, Ruth Manley, Lula Shelton, N. A. Winstead (investigator for law firm), Annie Reedy.

No one is required to make any statement but may make any statement that he or she sees fit. Investigation is conducted on the part of the State.

Some time ago, Mr. Smith Petty a citizen of Reidsville disappeared, we are informed, and I want now to ask any witness who may volunteer to state if he knows or if she knows where he is.

Joe Womack being questioned by Mr. Allen Gwyn
Q. Do you know Smith Petty
A. No
Q. Have you ever seen him?
A. Not that I know of
Q. Has any inquiry come to you in regard to his whereabouts?
A. Through two or three different sources it has been called to my attention that he was missing.
Q. Have you any knowledge as to his whereabouts?

A. No

Q. The information that you have comes from statements of others?

A. Yes

Sheriff J. F. Smith being questioned by Mr. Allen Gwyn

Q. Do you know Smith Petty

A. I am not personally acquainted with him

Q. Do you know him when you see him?

A. Yes

Q. Has he been to your town to your knowledge for the last several months?

A. He has not been here for some time.

Q. Do you know anything in regard to his whereabouts?

A. No

Q. Do you have any information in regard to his whereabouts?

A. Yes

Q. The information that you have comes then as a result of what you have been told

A. Yes

Mrs. John Price questioned by Mr. Allen Gwyn

Q. Do you know Smith Petty?

A. Yes

Q. When did you last see him?

A. I saw him some time since last October.

Q. Do you know where he was

A. Down around the Edna Cotton Mill. He tried to get a job there after it changed hands; after Mr. John Scott left the mill.

Q. Do you know today where he is?

A. No

Rev. Pardue questioned by Mr. Gwyn

Q. Do you know Smith Petty?

A. No

Q. Have you ever seen him?

A. Not that I know of.

Q. How long have you been living in Reidsville?

A. About three and one half months.

Q. How long have you been visiting Reidsville?

A. About two years

Q. Have you had any knowledge or information in regard to Mr. Smith Petty's whereabouts. Have you had any information as to his state or condition

A. I have no knowledge of it.

Q. I ask you on the part of the State and in the interest of the law to give any information that you have in regard to this, whether it is a matter that you desire to do or not.

A. Do you mean to ask me the question and do you mean for me to answer the question as to all the information I have received or heard

Q. I want you to give such information that you have that comes from reliable or most direct source

A. Mr. Gwyn, this is a matter that is not my choice to answer directly concerning this matter.

Q. But when the law calls upon you, Mr. Pardue, then it is your duty to give such information as you have.

A. Then you think, Mr. Gwyn as solicitor and attorney in this matter that it would be my duty to give such information and I am under obligation of the law to do such.

Q. The law places that upon every citizen, and I ask you to give such information as you have.

A. Personally, I had rather not make any statements in regard to it, but if you insist I am bound to give you such information as I have.

Q. I, as solicitor of Rockingham County, insist in the name of the law that you give me such information as you have.

Q. When did this matter first come to your attention?

A. About three months ago

Q. Where were you Mr. Pardue?

A. I was in Pinnix Warehouse.

Q. Who brought you the information?

A. Miss Alma Petty at that time.

Q. What was the occasion of your presence at the warehouse at that time?

A. Conducting a revival.

Q. Mr. Pardue, state in your own words as nearly as you can recall just what Miss Petty said to you.

A. When I was through my message one night, Miss Alma came to the altar for prayer and while a number of others came she lingered and I think we had dismissed the congregation. After a majority of the people had gone out, I was talking to Mr. Lillard down near the end of the choir loft and she came and said she wanted to speak to me. I said to her "I'll be through in just a moment and I'll speak to you". When I was through with the conversation with Mr. Lillard she and I walked up in the choir loft. She sat down in a chair and I sat down near by her. She said "I have a confession to make to you" and I said "alright". She said I am guilty of two of the biggest sins in the world. I said, "You know you are not" She said "Yes I am too". Then she said, do you think I can get forgiveness. I said, I don't know. I want to know what the sins are and then I will do all I can for you. She then asked me what the unpardonable sin was. I explained it to her. Then she said "I am guilty of murder and then I said "Oh I see" and I said "Where, in this town" and she said "yes" and I said "who" and if I'm not mistaken, she said "I can't tell you; then I said "I see" and she said "It is not what you think it is yet. I then asked her to tell me the whole truth. She said "I killed my father.

By Mr. Gwyn

Q. Mr. Pardue, how did she say she killed her father?

A. She didn't tell me at that time.

Q. Did you have another conversation with her.

A. Yes, a few days later down at my home.

Q. Go ahead and give the full details of the conversation between you and Miss Petty

A. After she told me that at the warehouse I never was so worried and unnerved in my life. I had always had a great interest in her. I couldn't sleep for thinking about it; then I went up to Dr. Meador's office one afternoon to talk to her about it and tell her what untold agony it brought me. When I got to the office, they were busy and I asked her to come to my house that afternoon. She said she and Blanche Moore would come the next evening. She came but Miss Moore did not come with her. I asked her to tell me the full details and that I would be more than glad to help her. She then sat down to my right.

Q. I insist that you go ahead and tell the full details. Were you and she by yourselves?

A. Yes

Q. You were alone in view of the fact that she had disclosures to make that she did not want the public to know?

A. Yes

Q. Mr. Pardue, what time of day was this?

A. About six or six thirty in the evening.

Q. Did she lead the conversation or did you?

A. Really I lead the conversation when we first begun talking.

Q. Mr. Pardue, I realize that it is a matter you would cast aside if you could do it, but that is not the question, notwithstanding the fact that you prefer not to tell this, I will have to insist that you tell me what took place.

Q. How did she say that she effected the killing?

A. She said she struck him a blow with an axe on top of the head.

Q. When did this take place and where?

A. If I am not mistaken, in the dining room. In the house near Mr. Sam Mitchell's on the corner.

Q. Go ahead and tell what she told you.

A. She said she came in home one Sunday evening and her father was whipping her mother, choking her, said then she proceeded to take her mother's part and in the fight, she was about to get the best of her father, but finally he got the best of her and gave her a whipping. Said then her father began to play the victrola and began to sing, did most everything that he could to contrary the family; that he went down in the basement in the night, took the axe and beat around down there and came back up stairs. The next morning about five o'clock she said she went down in the basement, brought the axe up stairs and intended to kill him then but she decided she would wait until they all went to work. I think she said they went to work and about seven o'clock she cooked breakfast. Mr. Petty got up to eat, came in cursing in the usual way. She prepared the cereal and he sat down and ate that. In the meantime she fixed the axe nearby the door so that she could get hold of it to use in the act. Said then she fixed the egg, placed it before him and as he began to eat the egg, she took the axe and made the first blow. His head fell over in the plate with blood streaming. After a minute he fell on the floor. He opened his eyes and said "Alma why are you trying to kill me" and then she struck him two more blows with the axe. He managed to get the axe from her and she then dragged him to the other room and realizing that some action must be taken at once, she got hold of a piece of iron pipe and finished him up with that.

Q. Did she say whether anyone was present in the house?

A. There was no one else present she said.

Q. What did she say she did with the body?

A. She said she put the body in her trunk in the closet in the dining room.

Q. Does that dining room have a closet

A. Yes

Q. How long did it stay there?

A. Two days.

Q. Then what became of it?

A. If I am not mistaken, she said a Dodge sedan drove up and carried the body away and they buried it

Q. Did she say whether the body was taken away in the day or night?

A. I am not positive about that.

Q. Did you ever see her anywhere else besides Reidsville?

A. Yes, in Winston-Salem.

Q. Did you ever see her in Leaksville?

A. Yes, a number of times and she always seemed to be interested in the scripture.

Q. Have you had any conversation with her since the one at your home in Reidsville?

A. No

Miss Blanche Moore questioned by Mr. Gwyn

Q. Miss Moore, how old are you?

A. Twenty

Q. How long have you known Alma?

A. Five or six years

Q. Have you heard anything in regard to Mr. Petty

A. What I know came as a result of what I heard.

Mrs. Alma Petty Gatlin questioned by Mr. Gwyn

Q. How old are you

A. 21 yesterday

Q. Where is your sister?

A. In Virginia, sick in bed.

Q. Your mother is dead, isn't she?

A. Yes, she died on March 9, 1927

Q. Your father was not at your home when your mother died, was he?

A. No

Q. How long have you known Mr. Pardue.

A. Ever since his first meetings held in Reidsville

Q. Did your father and mother ever have any quarrels?

A. Yes

Q. Did you take up for your mother?

A. Not any more than I had to.

Q. Was he mean to your mother.

A. Yes, he was mean to all of us.

Q. Do you know of his whereabouts.

A. I do not

Q. When was the last time he was at home?

A. The first of December, 1926

Q. Did you make any statement to Mr. Pardue in regard to your father?

A. I did not.

Q. Are the statements that Mr. Pardue just made true?

A. No, they are not.

Q. Never had any conversation with him about your father?

A. No

Q. Never mentioned your father to him.

A. No

Q. What kind of trunk do you have?

A. A blue trunk.

Q. How many other trunks do you have?

A. Two, old trunks.

Q. When did you marry?

A. July 7, 1927.

Q. Where were you living at the time of the disappearance of your father?

A. I don't know anything about it; we were living on Lindsey Street at the time he left home.

Q. Have you made any statement to Ruby Jasper*

A. No

Q. Did Ruby Jasper ever spend a night with you?

A. No, but I spent several with Ruby and several with Mrs. Jasper* when Ruby was out of town.

Q. When is the last time you spent the night with her?

A. I don't remember

Q. Did you make any statement to Ruby in regard to your father?

A. Nothing except that he was mean to us.

Q. Did Blanche Moore ever spend the night with you?

A. Yes

Q. Did she ever make the statement to you while she was at your house that she was afraid of anything?

A. No

Q. Did you ever make the statement to her that if she knew what you knew that she would be afraid?

A. No

Q. Where did your mother work?

A. Belk-Stevens Company

Q. How many children did your mother have?

A. Four living

Q. One dead?

A. None

Q. Wasn't she confined prior to her death

A. Yes, two months mis-carriage.

Q. Do you have a cedar chest in your home?

A. Yes, it was mother's.

Q. Was that child layed in the cedar chest?

A. No

Q. Didn't you make a statement to Blanche Moore that a child was layed in the chest and haven't you got materials now in that chest on which the child lay.

A. No

Q. Did you assist in disposing of the child?

A. I did it myself. My sister drove me out on the Lawsonville road and I buried it out there.

Q. In the night?

A. No

Q. Did you bury it on the right or left hand side of the road?

A. Why does it matter?

Q. I'll ask you if you buried it on the right or left hand side of the road?

A. On the left hand side

Q. How soon did this happen after your father disappeared?

A. He left home in December and this happened in March

Q. Your father was not at your mother's burial

A. No

Q. Do you have a closet in the dining room at the home where you used to live

A. No

Q. How long did you live in that house?

A. I don't remember, several months

Q. Then, you don't remember whether there are any closets in the house or not?

A. Yes, there were several in the house.

Q. Did you ever do any varnishing or painting in that house?

A. Yes, papa painted the floors.

Q. Where did you get your trunk?

A. It was mother's; I took it after she died; I never owned a trunk myself

Q. Have you made any inquiries as to where your father is?

A. Yes, some of his people were down here several weeks ago looking for him. I had Mr. Scott to run an ad in the Textile Bulletin for several months looking for him.

Q. Have you ever made the statement that you don't ever want to see your father any more?

A. I can't say that I have; I probably have.

Q. If you probably have made such a statement, is it because you didn't want to see him?

A. Yes, he has never been anything but a brute to me, why should I want to see him.

Q. Did your mother want to see him.

A. I don't know. She said several times in my presence that she would like to hear from him. He has left home several times like this, but we didn't think anything about it until lately.

Q. Your sister felt the same as you did about this matter, didn't she?

A. I have no idea how she felt.

Q. You did advertise for him then did you?

A. Yes

Q. Why did you advertise for him.

A. So he could help support the children

Q. Did you think that advertising would bring support from him?

A. Yes, I certainly did.

Q. How many brothers and sisters have you?

A. I have two small brothers and one sister.

Q. He didn't tell you where he was going?

A. No.

Mr. Eugene Gatlin questioned by Mr. Gwyn

Q. Have you heard the story as to the death of Smith Petty?

A. No

Q. Has anyone talked to you about it?

A. No.

Q. When is the first time you heard anything about it?

A. About two weeks ago a fellow told me up on the street that Mr.

Petty was missing; that there was a mystery to it and perhaps he had been murdered.

Q. Did you ask anybody else about it?

A. No

Q. Although you know that rumor has been out in town that he has been murdered, you didn't try to find out who murdered him or anything about it?

A. They didn't say he was murdered; they said he was missing, probably foul play. I asked my wife about it and she told me that her father left home about December 1st and she didn't know where he went and that was all there was to it.

Q. When was the first suggestion made to you?

A. Probably ten days or two weeks ago.

Q. You have heard from two or three sources about the rumor going around town?

A. Yes

Q. Who was the man who told you?

A. I rather not give his name now. I will tell you privately.

Q. Did he tell you that the matter was being investigated?

A. Yes, Mr. Lively came to me and said that he received a letter from an Insurance Company in regard to Mr. Petty's whereabouts and asked me what I knew about it.

Q. Then notwithstanding the fact that the matter was being discussed; that it was being investigated; that you asked your wife about it and she stated that your father-in-law had left home and you were not concerned further?

A. No, I didn't discuss it with her any more.

Q. How long have you been going with Alma?

A. Since last summer

Q. Did you know Mr. Petty.

A. I never met him. The last time I saw him he was engaged in a fight at the Reidsville Lunch in the Fall of 1926.

Q. Do you know whether there was a child born in their home or not?

A. Just now was the first I had heard of it.

Q. You didn't know her condition when she died?

A. Houston Saunders (a local undertaker) told me the day she was buried that was her trouble.

Q. And you had never made any suggestion to your wife about that?

A. No

Q. Do you know when she was buried?

A. Yes

Q. Do you know whether Mr. Petty was at the funeral or not?

A. I didn't see him.

Q. Did you assist around the home when she died?

A. Yes

Q. Did it occur to you why he didn't come to the funeral?

A. No.

Q. Did she attempt to find him when her mother died?

A. No more than telegrams I sent for her to Franklinton, N. C. and one to Gastonia.

Q. Through what office?

A. Western Union.

Q. When.

A. The morning of March 10th.

Rev. Pardue questioned by Mr. Gwyn

Q. What statement, if any, did Alma make to you in regard to what she would say if her confession were divulged?

A. I said "Alma if this is a matter you want cleared up between you and your God you must come clean to the authorities, and she said "I'll not do it". I told her that some day I might be questioned about it and she said "if you tell what I have told you, I'll deny it".

Mrs. Alma Petty Gatlin questioned by Mr. Gwyn

Q. Alma, did you ever talk to Mr. Pardue in the meetings?

A. Yes, several times.

Q. Did you have an axe in your home?

A. Yes

Q. Did you ever fix your father's breakfast?

A. No, I never did any cooking.

Q. How long have you been working?

A. About four years

Q. Does your sister work?

A. No, she is not working now; she used to sell tickets at the Grand Theater.

Q. You didn't have to go to work as early as the other members of your family did, did you?

A. I go to work at 8:30.

Q. Did you ever stay at home after your mother left to go to her work?

A. No, I usually went on to work as she did.

Q. You never fried an egg?
A. Yes, I guess I have in my life.
Q. Prior to your mother's death did you do the cooking?
A. No
Q. Did you ever prepare a meal for your father?
A. No
Q. Never in your life?
A. I have assisted mother in preparing meals for him.
Q. How many times have you heard it said that your father met with foul play?
A. My husband told me one time that he heard it discussed on the streets that my father was missing.
Q. People had told him that your father had been murdered and he did not discuss it with you?
A. No

Mr. Eugene Gatlin questioned by Mr. Gwyn
Q. After people told you and after it had been suggested to you that your father in law had met with foul play, did you not tell your wife what you heard?
A. I only asked her if she knew where he was and she said no and we didn't discuss it any more.
Q. Did you know of your own knowledge where he was?
A. No.
Q. Can you explain why you didn't ask your wife about these rumors? Were you afraid of her?
A. I mentioned it to her and she said that he had left home, but she didn't know where he was.

Mrs. Alma Petty Gatlin questioned by Mr. Gwyn
Q. Do you know Mr. Pou
A. Yes, he used to go with my sister.
Q. Where is he now?
A. I don't know
Q. Do you know where he lives.
A. I don't know the name of the place, somewhere in Virginia.
Q. Has your sister ever heard from him since he left?
A. Yes, she has gotten several cards from him.
Q. Where were the cards sent from.
A. I don't know, I didn't notice.

Q. When did you have the last difficulty with your father?

A. There was a fuss just before he left the last time. Said he was going away and that he would never return.

Q. On his last trip here, did he slap anybody.

A. Yes

Q. Did he slap you.

A. Yes

Q. How many times did he slap you?

A. A half dozen times I guess.

Q. Did you slap him back?

A. No

Q. Did you ever threaten to kill him?

A. No

Q. Was he dangerous?

A. Yes, several times he carried a knife around with him. He borrowed a pistol and told us he was going to kill us while we were asleep.

Q. When he was here last, how many times did he threaten to kill you all?

A. I don't remember.

Q. When did he have the fight at the Reidsville Lunch?

A. I didn't know anything about it.

Q. Miss Alma, do you think this is a funny matter?

A. No, I realize it is serious.

Q. You are smiling, do you think it is a matter to smile about?

A. If I did, I would smile.

Q. Is there any other statement that you wish to make about this matter?

A. Well, I don't understand any of it; I don't know what they are all talking about. I don't understand Mr. Pardue's statements.

Q. Is there anything you want to say in regard to Mr. Pardue's statements?

A. Nothing, except deny them.

Mrs. John Price questioned by Mr. Gwyn

Q. Mrs. Price is there any statement you wish to make in regard to this?

A. No

End of transcript

• • •

Even though she'd had little to say at Solicitor Gwyn's investigation, just being a part of it had made Mrs. Price nervous. Then, only three days after the inquiry, she had been horrified by the sheriff's discovery of Smith Petty's body buried in the basement of the house that she and her husband had rented from the owner, Squire D. E. Purcell, after the Pettys moved. The whole time they were living there, Petty's body had been slowly rotting away under the coal pile. The thought of it tore Mrs. Price up, but she got herself together well enough to do her duty as one of the people who had known Smith Petty and were called upon to identify his body while it still lay exposed in its shallow grave in the basement.

The gruesome sight and the awful stench were almost more than she could endure. And in her basement! But it sure wasn't going to be her basement much longer. Her husband John was having as big a fit as she was to get out of there, so they had hurriedly gathered a few pieces of clothing and left that place for good. The furniture could wait; they'd worry about it later.

They had registered that afternoon at the Belvedere Hotel, right across the street from Wilkerson Funeral Home. By mid-winter, newspapermen from cities all across the state would have rooms in the hotel. The stories they were to file would put Reidsville on the map. And nearby Wentworth, too, for that was the location of the county jail and the courthouse where the trial would be held.

Although he had moved across the railroad with the rest of his family after the death of his mother, Alma's younger brother, Smith, often would return to the old neighborhood to see his playmate, G. W. Windsor. During the course of the trial, the two boys were to brave cold rain and sleet and make their way to the *Reidsville Review* office, where each would pick up a bundle of newspapers and trudge down the hill to the cigarette factory.

G. W. would recall sixty-four years later that they would stand at the employees' entrance on Oakes Alley and catch the workers leaving the plant. He said they always hollered "extra," like the newsboys did in the picture shows; didn't make any difference whether they were really extras or not. Alma was always in the headlines and her little brother and his friend were selling the papers, so they never failed to sell out.

9

By the sixth day of Alma's incarceration, while Solictor Gwyn was examining, among other witnesses, Alma's sister, Thelma, and her nine-year-old brother, Smith, a decided change seemed to have come over the prisoner. Gone was the happy and unconcerned attitude of her first few days in jail. She appeared extremely worried, and some expressed the opinion that they wouldn't be surprised if she suffered a complete breakdown any time and told everything she knew about the murder of her father. There was much speculation about what she might say: Would she confess that she acted alone and committed the crime? Or would she implicate others?

The speculation proved groundless. After eleven days behind bars, Alma was her old lighthearted self again. Far from being a candidate for a nervous breakdown, she gave every evidence of doing remarkably well and often joked with jail attendants as well as the inmates. Her friends kept her cell filled with fresh flowers and, in spite of the loss of one of her two love birds a few days earlier, she hid her grief behind a cheerful smile. And when a mirror was broken on the same day, she refused to let a silly superstition upset her.

Jailer John W. Irving, with a reputation for being kind and considerate to all his prisoners, however poor and unfortunate, had been besieged by nearly a thousand people on the previous Sunday, but all requests to see Alma were refused and only close relatives and two of her attorneys were allowed to see her. However, magazines and flowers from interested visitors were sent to her.

When questioned by the press, Alma's lawyers all had the

same answer: They would have a few surprises, come trial time. And soon P. W. Glidewell was confidently predicting that at the trial's end, when the jury had returned its verdict, he would drive Alma back to Reidsville on the front seat of his car, a free woman.

Perhaps the optimism expressed by her chief counsel further lifted Alma's spirits and prompted her to write *The Review* a letter which appeared in the Monday, September 26, 1927 issue under the heading: MRS. GATLIN IS CHEERFUL. She expressed her thanks for their sending *The Review* to her in Wentworth. She said that reading it was next to being right in Reidsville and she truly enjoyed each word of it. Alma included one of her original poems "to be published if they cared to do so," and the poem was printed with her letter. Many more poems were to be written during the long months she remained in jail awaiting trial, and *The Review* would print all of them. Alma was later to mention the possibility of publishing a book of her poems.

Alma continued to maintain her innocence and would dismiss with a shrug any reference to the confession the preacher alleged she had made to him. She had no idea where he got all that stuff from, she would say with a smile that implied that he must have made it up to get his picture in the paper.

In spite of Alma's popularity, many people chose to believe that Rev. Pardue was telling the truth and Alma was guilty as sin. Others were equally sure she was innocent, and there were a few women so completely convinced of Alma's innocence that they carried in their purses a copy of one of her poems, clipped from *The Reidsville Review*. Nobody who could write such a sweet poem about their mother could possibly kill anybody, they argued adamantly, offering the clipping as proof that she couldn't any more kill her father than she could kill her mother. The only trouble was everybody in town had already read the poem, which appears below. But even if they hadn't already seen it, that wouldn't have changed anything. Like people arguing politics, their minds were already made up.

While Alma Petty Gatlin had sat in her cell at the Rockingham County Jail in mid-September, awaiting trial in Wentworth, Ruth Snyder and her lover, Judd Gray, were being examined at Sing Sing Prison by the lunacy commission and found sane.

MOTHER

The first word I learned to say,
The one I saw first every day,
The one who kissed my tears away,
That blessed one was mother!
One who loved me all the time,
Not ere a thought was in her mind
Except to be so good and kind.
Dear loving mother!
She who taught me how to pray,
How in kindness to repay
Even friends who would betray,
Blessed sainted mother!
Always ready to sacrifice
Always ready to pay the price,
Always loving kind and nice
That one was mother!
How thankful I shall always be
That God gave her, just to me,
And at the end, I will be
With my precious mother!
Though she's gone, she lingers still
My darkest hours with joy she fills
Happiness comes that I can't conceal
With memories of my mother!

ALMA PETTY GATLIN
Written October 3, 1927

Rev. Pardue had told newspapermen that when he asked Alma during her alleged confession last May how she had killed her father, she replied "it was another Gray-Snyder case." The evangelist said he was horrified by the comparison, since for some time the newspapers had been full of sensational stories about the clumsy though brutal murder of Albert Snyder in his Queens, Long Island, home by his wife Ruth and her secret lover, Judd Gray. Ruth Snyder, a thirty-two-year-old bored housewife, who longed to be a "red-hot mama," had to finish the job begun by her "lover boy." Judd Gray, a mild-mannered corset salesman, succeeded only in waking up Snyder when he hit the sleeping spouse over the head with a sash weight. Coming to the aid of her lover, Ruth knocked her husband unconscious with the sash weight, then chloroformed him, and finally strangled him with picture wire until at last he was dead.

The crime was committed on March 20, 1927, and by the time the case went to trial each was vehemently blaming the other, with many well-known personalities, including evangelists Billy Sunday and Aimee Semple McPherson, present in the courtroom. Found guilty, Judd Gray and Ruth Snyder died in the electric chair at Sing Sing on the bleak night of January 12, 1928.

Newspapers the next day all carried accounts of their executions. It was big news, since Ruth Snyder was the first woman ever electrocuted. Reading about it surely must have caused Alma Petty Gatlin to reflect on her own mortality, for she was scheduled to go on trial for her life in less than two weeks.

The trial date had been set for January 23, with Judge Thomas J. Shaw of Guilford presiding. But with both sides ready to go, they were to be disappointed when the case was ordered to be continued until the next term of court in February.

Rev. Pardue, though none too anxious to appear as a witness, had been ready to be called. Now he would have to wait. However, it was Alma Gatlin who would be most adversely affected. With the trial set to begin on February 13, she would spend three more long weeks in jail agonizing over her fate. At least, so it would seem; though her lawyers and the jailer were all to insist that she remained in good spirits.

P. T. Stiers was the first lawyer hired to defend Alma, but P. W. Glidewell had become her chief defense attorney. In addition to P.

70

T. Stiers and P. W. Glidewell, Alma had another Reidsville lawyer, F. Eugene Hester, as well as Attorney A. W. Dunn, who was Glidewell's partner in the firm's Leaksville office.

Two of Alma's four lawyers were reputed to be womanizers, but that didn't bother Alma as long as they kept their hands off her. However, according to a rumor making the rounds, one of them hadn't been able to keep his hands to himself, prompting Alma to request of the jailer that this particular lecherous lawyer not be allowed in her cell unless one of her other lawyers was also present. If that wasn't possible, she asked that the jailer position himself so that he could watch from the door and make sure she was not subjected to any further attempts to fondle her.

Although P. W. Glidewell was listed as Alma's chief counsel, the talk downtown was that soft-spoken P. T. Stiers did the thinking and P. W. Glidewell did the talking. Daddy chuckled when he told Mama about it and remarked that it would make P. W. mad as fire if he knew what they were saying.

There were indeed many people who regarded P. T. Stiers as the shrewder lawyer of the two, although they readily admitted that P. W. Glidewell's courtroom style and his oratorical powers were hard to beat.

P. W. was well aware of the importance of his uncanny instinct for knowing exactly when to slip into his down-to-earth-country-lawyer approach and talk to the jury like he was one of them. But it was his eloquence as an orator that he was especially vain about, so much so that he was to succumb one morning to the flattery of a spectator who would arrive too late to get a seat at Alma's trial. The woman would tell Mr. Glidewell that she had always heard what a wonderful speaker he was but had never had the opportunity to hear him plead a case. P. W. would beam and turn to the bailiff. "It would be a shame to disappoint this nice young lady here, wouldn't it, bailiff?" Almost immediately four chairs would be magically produced for the lady and her three friends, and to their great delight, placed right in front of the bar. The woman was to tell her daughters years later that she couldn't believe that a lawyer of P. W. Glidewell's stature would be so susceptible to flattery that it would get them ringside seats for the most dramatic trial ever held in Rockingham County.

Smith Petty's father, John, right. Other man likely his
son. L.O. Petty. (Photo courtesy N.C. Collection,
UNC Library at Chapel Hill)

10

Still grieving over the bad news he had received the day before at his home in Union, South Carolina, John Petty arrived in Reidsville Sunday morning, determined to visit his granddaughter in her prison cell in Wentworth before the funeral that afternoon. He thought he could persuade Alma to tell him if somebody had helped her murder his son, but that proved as hopeless as a drowning man grabbing at a straw.

Although he couldn't get her to tell him, he was already sure who her accomplice would turn out to be. He just wanted to hear her say it.

Alma had already denied at the solicitor's investigation that she ever confessed anything at all to Rev. Pardue, and she curtly informed her grandfather that she had nothing more to say about the charge.

She could deny that she had killed his boy until doomsday, but the white-haired old man would never believe her. He left the jail unconvinced that a preacher would have made up such a story.

Smith Petty's funeral was held on Sunday, September 4, the day after his body was found in the basement. With three of his murdered son's brothers at his side, grief-stricken John Petty showed no signs of seeing or hearing anything as he sat with bowed head at the feet of Rev. Pardue, who stood on a box while he conducted the service. It must have added to the old man's sadness to be struck with the realization that only a relative handful of people out of the crowd of hundreds gathered on the lawn of Wilkerson Funeral Home were there to pay their sincere last respects to Smith Petty. Most had come not out of any respect for his dead son but solely out of morbid curiosity. They didn't care anything about his boy when he was alive and he had the nagging notion that they didn't really care that he was dead.

John Petty's bitterness had so clouded his judgment that he found it hard to believe that there might still be a few caring people left in the world.

Mrs. L. L. Moore was a person who cared. A kindly lady who loved people, she enjoyed doing for her family and never minded when her children unexpectedly brought friends home to eat with them. She set a good table and always made sure there was enough for unannounced company, invariably made to feel right at home.

Since Mrs. Moore's daughter, Blanche, and Alma had been friends, and her married daughter, Sudie Price, knew Smith Petty well when he was an overseer at the cotton mill where she worked in the office, it seemed the neighborly thing to do to invite Alma's grandfather and her uncles to have a meal with them. It was probably one of the few kindnesses shown the old man and his three sons while they were in town.

People admitted it was awful of them to laugh later about the hymn sung at the funeral but they couldn't help themselves. The truth was that every person present would have been distressed at the thought that John Petty or his sons might have realized too late to do anything about having included "Amazing Grace," with its inappropriately appropriate words, "I once was lost, but now am found."

It was hot everywhere the afternoon of the funeral, even under the huge oak trees that shaded the lawn of the funeral home on the southeast corner of Main and Gilmer Streets. The undertaker had no choice but to have the services in the open. They had tried everything from disinfectants to formaldehyde. Some said they even tried lime, the chemical used in the many outhouses still to be found in town, but they couldn't get rid of the smell. The large casket where the remains were encased lay in the garage until time for the funeral, when it was placed twenty feet beyond where the preacher stood.

After the singing of "Amazing Grace," he read from the 15th chapter of First Corinthians the verses that dealt with the resurrection; then he spoke for approximately fifteen minutes about Judgment Day and what a great day it would be when people of all nations stood before God and the secrets of the heart of all mankind would be revealed.

While her father's funeral was in progress, Alma, alone with the secrets in her heart, reclined on a small cot in her prison cell, seemingly indifferent to the wrath of her grandfather and his sons. It was even whispered about that Alma had expressed interest in seeing her father's remains, the same remains that gave off such a stifling stench that even the closed casket couldn't contain the odor that rose up and filled the nostrils of the pallbearers.

In those days, the lid of the coffin was simply dropped into place, like the hinged lid on an old Victrola. With no seal on the casket, it was easy on a hot day for the odor to escape from the wooden box.

John Pettigrew was one of the pallbearers and he didn't mind telling me, almost sixty-four years later, that the smell had made him sick; so sick that he wasn't up to going to the cemetery for the burial.

He wasn't ashamed of it. Not then, and not when we talked about it a few months before his death in September of 1991, just four days before his ninety-second birthday. John simply was not the kind of man who ever felt the need to prove himself. Though not a tall man, he always had the reputation of being all man, and for twelve years he was a tough police detective whose Buick was stepped-up to do 120 miles per hour. That was how he caught so many liquor cars

John Pettigrew, one of Smith Petty's pallbearers, as he looked in his nineties.

before he left the Reidsville Police Force in 1940. In the next nine years he was elected constable three times. At almost fifty years old and grown tired of his twenty-one years in law enforcement, he went back to the work he had done as a youth in his teens, before his eight-year stint at the American Tobacco Company: John Pettigrew went back to work for Edna Cotton Mill. Behind him was the wanderlust of his early years when, like Smith Petty, he had worked in mills all over the South. This time, John stayed put until he retired in 1964.

Nobody knew what prompted the young man in a small car to park near the funeral home lawn and blow his horn relentlessly that Sunday, disrupting the services for Smith Petty. The preacher interrupted his sermon and called on the police to correct the problem, which they did. The honking stopped and the young man drove away.

If the incident had happened in the '90s, it probably would have been assumed that the driver was trying to make some kind of statement. But in 1927, life was simpler and people were more naive than analytical. They were more interested in the welfare of the girl who fainted from the heat and had to be carried through the crowd to the open air than they were in the identity or motivation of some young buck honking his horn.

To John Petty, asking Rev. Pardue to preach his son's funeral was proper and fitting, since it was the preacher who took the initiative and saw to it that the murder of Smith Petty was brought to light. Rising to the challenge of conducting with dignity the funeral of a man about to be buried for the second time, Pardue assiduously avoided introducing any sensationalism into the services and made no direct reference to the crime or to Alma Petty Gatlin. However, he did use the slaying as an opportunity to appeal to evildoers and remind them that death could strike without warning. He prayed for compassion and sympathy for John Petty and delayed until the end of the prayer any reference to the murder and Alma's alleged confession. Careful to keep the reference indirect, he beseeched the Lord to bestow upon him the strength to expose evil and concluded his prayer with the fervent plea that God continue to bless him with a conscience that would allow no wrongdoing to remain concealed. As John Petty had requested, the service ended with the singing of "Nearer My God To Thee."

· · ·

76

When the old man had learned that the dead man was to be buried beside his wife, he was quick to protest, saying "If I had known she was buried here, I would have had Smith buried somewhere else." But it was already settled and beyond his control.

It seemed to John Petty the same lack of consideration shown when none of them had had the common decency to let him know that his son was missing from home in December. He didn't find out about it until one of his other sons, O. F. Petty, came to Reidsville from his home in Kannapolis to attend the funeral of Smith's wife in March and learned that his brother had disappeared.

Although Rev. Pardue announced that there would be no committal service held at the grave, the curiosity of the crowd was not sated: They wanted to be sure they didn't miss anything; they had to see it all, right down to the last clod of red clay mounded on top of the new grave. Almost as many people gathered at Greenview Cemetery, about a mile away, as had been present at the funeral home. After the coffin was lowered into the ground, John Petty stood beside his sons and looked down at the pine box. Those close enough to understand heard the broken old man mutter, "How could such a thing ever happen to my boy?" He could have added that nobody seemed to care except him and Smith's brothers.

The paucity of floral tributes was indeed a sad sight: a sheaf of artificial wheat and a bouquet of dahlias from the father and brothers placed on top of the raw red earth after the new grave had been spaded down. Though hundreds of people attended the funeral, those two floral offerings were all that had been sent.

John Petty hung back and didn't leave the cemetery with his three sons until everybody else was gone. He wanted to be shed of those curiosity seekers who might as well have been at a sideshow for all they cared about his boy.

II

Although I had known everybody in the Petty household by sight, I never knew them as well as I did our closer Lindsey Street neighbors. I played all around that house and in the holler behind it, but I can't remember ever going inside the house while the Pettys lived there. I was in the basement many times, though, when we were playing hide-and-go-seek. Later, I was to shudder with my playmates over what we hadn't known: Just a few feet from Mr. Petty's shallow grave ran the pipe that carried water to the spigot we drank from when we got hot and thirsty.

After the Petty home was empty and had become the famous Murder House, I was in it a lot of times. From the hallway, a long skeleton key could be seen protruding from the keyhole on the front door, and I used to wonder why the key was on the inside, since there was nobody in there to lock the door behind them. Unless you believed the story that the house was haunted. I never believed it, but most of the kids who attended Franklin Street Graded School were convinced it really was haunted. You didn't have to ask them; all you had to do was watch them going home after school. Just about every one would cross Lindsey Street to the Primitive Baptist Church side. Even in the daytime they didn't want to walk on the same side of the street where the Petty House was. Clark Holt, a Reidsville attorney, told me that twenty years after the murder, the Petty House was still being avoided by his generation of school kids, steeped in stories heard at home about the ax murder and the body in the basement.

G. W. Windsor and Sammy Mitchell were adventurous boys

and braver than the other kids. Each accepting the other's dare, they had taken their costumes with them to the spooky basement on Halloween night and dressed by flickering candlelight while they shivered near the hole where Mr. Petty's body had been found less than two months earlier. Dressed in sheets, the two boys succeeded in scaring out of their wits several youngsters who heard moans coming from the basement and cautiously ventured down the slope to peer in the basement door, whereupon out would leap the ghost of Smith Petty and another ghost brandishing a blood-dripping ax, a frighteningly realistic prop created by dousing the ax blade with ketchup.

Sixty-four years later, G. W. would remember the corner where the Petty house sat as the darkest, scariest spot in the neighborhood. The street light suspended over the middle of the intersection of Lindsey and Irvin Streets was so ineffectual that its feeble rays were completely swallowed up by the dark on the lower side of the Crutchfield's front yard, where there stood a huge ancient tree, time-fattened with thick vines that twisted into ghostly shapes in the night. Just across Franklin Street, the small Petty house was all but invisible in the inky blackness, but its presence loomed large and menacing in the imaginations of the young, for it was known to be the place where a bloody murder had

The Petty house on Franklin Street, where
Smith Petty's body was found in the basement

been committed with an ax that some said was borrowed from Sammy Mitchell's daddy's woodpile, right next door.

A number of newspapers ran a picture of the Petty House with the story about the discovery of the murdered man's body in the basement, so every pretty weekend would bring carloads of curious out-of-towners who just had to see the Murder House. But the tours I soon found myself conducting were not something I planned. They just happened.

The first time was on a Sunday afternoon. I was sitting on the rock wall that held up our front yard, enjoying the warm September sunshine, when a car with a Virginia license tag slowed to a stop and a lady in the back seat asked if I knew where the Murder House was. I told her yes ma'am and pointed out the house on the corner.

She thanked me, and just as the car started to pull away, I heard myself saying, "I was there when they dug him up." The driver hit his brakes and leaned out the car window. "You say you was there? Can you go over there and show us?" I told the man I'd be glad to.

After I showed them where I had watched from the basement window while they dug Mr. Petty's body up, we walked to the back of the house and went into the basement, so they could get a good look at the hole. Then I took them inside to show them the bloodstains on the floor in the closet where the trunk had leaked. I told them about the mysterious Dodge that had taken the trunk away with the body inside, but whoever it was got cold feet and brought it back.

I took them through the kitchen to the back porch and we looked down the steep steps that led to the lower back porch with its entrance to the basement, and I explained that most people thought that was the route taken to carry the body into the basement, because there would be less likelihood of being seen back there in the dark of night. I told them that it looked to me like it would be just as safe and a whole lot easier to wait until two or three o'clock in the morning when everybody was asleep and let the body out the window on the west side of the house, and then just push it through the basement window, the one I had looked through while the sheriff's men were digging the body up.

I wound up my spiel by saying that however they got Mr. Petty's body down there, somebody had been smart enough to order a load of coal to camouflage the grave.

The man from Virginia called me a regular little detective and asked me if I thought Alma had done it. I gave him the same answer I'd heard my daddy use and told him I reckoned that was something the jury would have to decide. The man grinned and pressed a quarter into my hand. At first, I refused, but he insisted that I take it. It was worth it, he said. So I took the quarter and I thanked him. And that was the way I got started on the tours.

I made a whole lot of quarters that fall and on up until the weather started getting bad. I had to quit then anyway, because when Mama found out what I was doing, she made me stop; said it was disrespectful to be making money off of poor Mr. Petty. Mama may have been the only person who ever called him anything as kindly as "poor Mr. Petty" after his murder was discovered and the stories came out about the mistreatment his family had suffered at his hands.

The Reidsville Review had stated in its September 9, 1927 issue that Smith Petty "seems to have been the sort of fellow that leaves the world no poorer by dying." A mild appraisal compared to typical descriptions of the murdered man in most of the newspapers: A poor provider and a heavy drinker, a violent man who abused his family on his infrequent visits home.

Although it would have been hard in those days to find anybody who would agree, Smith Petty had his good side. It is more correct to say that he once had his good side; for "up until the time that Alma reached about fifteen or sixteen, she was foolish about her daddy" according to Ruby Hopper, a friend with whom she exchanged Pollyanna Christmas presents at Sunday school. Now Mrs. Ruby Delancey, she has kept all these years two of Alma's gifts to her: a glass decanter with an etched floral design and a ceramic Easter Bunny holding an egg.

While waiting for the completion of the building that would be his first church, Preacher Pardue held services in temporary quarters in the Union Warehouse on Settle Street and was gratified by the consistently large turnouts. And on Sunday, September 11, just over a week after the body of Smith Petty was found, a crowd of one thousand people had gathered to watch Rev. Thunderbolt Tom Pardue baptize thirteen people in the "Baptizing Hole" in the curve of Haw River near Lewis Bridge, about eight miles south of Reidsville.

The preacher surely realized that it was his notoriety that had drawn such a huge crowd to the baptizing, and in his heart of hearts he must have secretly admitted to himself that there was more than just a touch of the opportunist in his ministry. He probably salved his conscience by reminding himself that he couldn't save lost souls unless he could get people to come to his services.

With editorials and letters to newspaper editors about evenly divided on the issue of ethical questions raised by his actions, Rev. Pardue was heartened by the testimonial given him by the members of his new church when they voted their belief that he had done right. But he realized that he was still the target of much criticism from the clergy and that for every minister who supported him for acting on his conscience and taking Alma's story to the authorities, there was another who censored him for betraying the confidentiality of the penitent.

There seemed to be no middle ground on the general public's opinion of Pardue. People either loved him or they hated him. One regular churchgoer who truly loved the Lord would forget her Christianity at the mere mention of Pardue's name. She hated his sensationalism and antics in the pulpit so much she couldn't stand to hear his name. But the very things she so despised were what brought others to his tabernacle to hear him preach the old-time religion with enthusiastic fervor.

T. Jeff Penn didn't give a damn what anybody said about Tom Pardue; in his opinion, he was a good man and a conscientious man. T. Jeff liked the preacher, admired his dedication, and was quick to say so.

Although most people saw only the blustery side of T. Jeff Penn, the preacher recognized him as the kind and caring person he really was. A short, stocky man with a ruddy complexion and a gruff way of talking, the Reidsville millionaire fooled a lot of people, but not Rev. Pardue. The preacher knew that Mr. Penn's brusqueness was largely an affectation cultivated to camouflage his tenderheartedness. To prove his point, Pardue related a story about his benefactor:

"I had closed a service, to go home and spend the night with my wife," the evangelist said, "when my song leader handed me a note which said 'Dear Mister Pardue: So that we may know that we do good as the days come and go, you'll find my check here for just fifty-one dollars. Just ten times the amount that a penitent one gave back to me, which he confessed he stole a few years ago; one of your converts.'

"The note was from Mister Penn, and reading it and looking at the check, I'll never forget how I felt. I fell right in the floor - prostrate - and thanked the Lord. It was a joy to me, to know that Jeff Penn recognized the worth of my work. One of his men had stolen five dollars and ten cents from him and he gave me ten times the amount that had been stolen from him years before.

"Later on I was passing by and just stepped in his office and he asked me how I was getting along with my church down there, and I told him we were doing pretty good. He asked about my salary and I said, 'Well, they're poor people down there and they're doing about all they can.' He turned around to his secretary and said, 'Write Mister Pardue a check for fifty dollars.'"

The minister concluded the story by stating that he wanted to show his appreciation, so he had gone down to T. Jeff Penn's church and preached the next Sunday. But he did not mention that it was the Church of Christ, the same church where Alma Petty Gatlin had been such an active member.

Rev. Pardue's considerable publicity as Alma Petty Gatlin's accuser had stirred up a controversy that raged in editorials and stories in newspapers up and down the eastern seaboard. Laymen and clergymen agreed and disagreed in print on the ethics of a preacher's betrayal of the penitent's confidentiality, while legal minds were more concerned over the admissibility of the alleged confession as evidence.

The trial would pit accuser against accused. The word of an evangelistic preacher who was both loved and despised against the word of a popular young bride. Expected to be full of fireworks and surprises, the trial was to pack people in every day of its ten-day run.

12

Smith Petty's father, John Petty, arrived in Reidsville from his home in Union, South Carolina on Sunday afternoon, January 22, 1928. Traveling alone, the elderly man had come by train to attend the trial of his granddaughter in Wentworth, hoping to take the witness stand against her for the state. But John Petty's first trip to Reidsville since the funeral of his son in September was to be cut short and he would return home disappointed.

On Monday, with the courtroom filled to capacity, Major T. Smith, Clerk of Superior Court, swore in the members of the Grand Jury, with H. E. Link as foreman. After instructions from Judge Thomas J. Shaw, the Grand Jury retired for deliberation.

When the Grand Jury returned in a body with their foreman, each of the eighteen jurors polled individually stated that he found a true bill against Alma Petty Gatlin on the charge of murder.

With the indictment of his granddaughter accomplished, it seemed to John Petty, anxious for the trial to get under way, that the stage was set and the courtroom drama was about to begin. But it was not to happen that day.

S. Porter Graves, Solicitor of the Superior Court District, who would prosecute the case with information fed him by Rockingham Solicitor Allen H. Gwyn, suggested that some decision be rendered regarding the congested condition of the court calendar. Judge Shaw's response, after discussing the matter with Chief Defense Attorney P. W. Glidewell and Solicitor Graves, was to order the case continued until the next term of court. Although no mention was made of it, Judge Cameron F. MacRae would be presiding at the February term.

All John Petty could do was shake his white head. Nothing to do but go back to Union, South Carolina and return to his job as a night watchman. He'd just have to wait until next month and then make another trip to North Carolina. He aimed to be right there when Alma went on trial, and, as he was quick to say, if his granddaughter was guilty, "he hoped full punishment would be meted out to her."

John Petty was as good as his word. He was indeed right there, sitting in the courtroom on Monday morning, February 13, with his son, L. O. Petty, of Kannapolis, North Carolina, at his side, when Alma Petty Gatlin was brought into court at 11:30 to be formally arraigned on the charge of murdering her father.

At the same moment that Alma came in through the door to the right of the bench, Rev. Pardue appeared at the rear of the courtroom. As though trying to get his bearings, he glanced about until he finally spotted a vacant seat in the press box. As he slid into the seat, he whispered to the reporters that Alma wasn't nearly as fat as she had been and looked like she had lost about forty pounds since she confessed to him. Nobody answered.

The solicitor stood and turned toward Alma, instructing her to stand up before he began to read the formal indictment charging that Alma Petty Gatlin "with malice aforethought and premeditation, killed and murdered her father against the statutes made and provided and against the peace and dignity of the state."

In a ringing voice, the solicitor asked, "Alma Petty Gatlin, how do you plead — guilty or not guilty?"

"Not guilty, sir," she answered evenly, looking the solicitor squarely in the eye, as she had throughout the reading of the indictment.

Sitting motionless among the newsmen, his face pale, Rev. Pardue swallowed uncomfortably.

"How will you be tried?" the solicitor continued.

"By God and my country," she answered without wavering.

"May He send you a true deliverance," said the solicitor, concluding the arraignment.

When court opened Tuesday morning, the courthouse was filled to overflowing. A huge crowd milled around outside, though there was no chance of their getting inside the building, since even the outer halls were packed.

Necks began to crane as Alma Petty Gatlin was brought into

the courtroom at 9:45. She seemed calm, in spite of blinking her eyes from time to time, a tic she'd had since her school days, as recalled by her classmate Mutt Burton. She had on the same tan full-length coat with a fur collar she had worn the day before when she was arraigned. Wearing a dark blue dress, she held in her hand a single red rose. Pinned on her shoulder was a nosegay of lively colored yarns, resembling those made by ladies at their sewing circles, none of which Alma's mother had ever been interested in joining.

Helen Trent, owner of the first beauty parlor in Reidsville, had paid a professional visit over the weekend to the jail, where she trimmed and washed Alma's dark bobbed hair, leaving it soft and lustrous.

The defendant wore no rouge and only a touch of lipstick. So perhaps it was by design that Alma looked pale and somewhat sad as she took her place between her little brother, nine-year-old Smith Petty, and her husband Eugene Gatlin, Reidsville fire chief, who was on a leave of absence for the duration of the trial.

With her four lawyers in attendance, Alma, who had said she would like to be tried by a jury from her own county and that "if there were any women taken on these juries, she would like to have some of them," watched and listened with interest, sometimes whispering to her lawyers, as the important process of jury selection dragged along.

Alma may have been lucky that no women were summoned for jury duty. Until recently, Alma seemed to have considerable sympathy from the public, but when the talk began that she had written stories for *True Story* magazine, many of the holier-than-thou sisters in the churches turned against her, in spite of Alma's denials of having written for the mildly racy magazine.

Sheriff J. F. Smith had had his deputies traveling miles and miles of Rockingham County's sleet-covered roads the previous day as they rounded up the two hundred men summoned to appear at the Wentworth Courthouse as the Special Venire from which the jury was to be drawn.

Solicitor Graves and Attorney Glidewell argued back and forth about the competency of questions each fired at the veniremen until, finally, at 10:30 a.m., J. B. Albert, a twenty-seven-year-old farmer from Huntsville township, was accepted for jury duty. He was the third one called.

The eleventh man called, J. W. Corum, a farmer of Reidsville

Rockingham County
Solicitor Allen H.
Gwyn.
(Photo courtesy Russ
Gwyn Robertson.

Surry County Solicitor
Porter Graves.
(Photo courtesy
Historical Collection
Room, Rockingham
Community College)

Left to right, P.W. Glidewell, chief attorney for the defense,
Smith Petty, Jr., Alma Petty Gatlin, Woodrow Petty,
Thelma Petty, top center.
(Photo courtesy N.C. Collection,
UNC Library at Chapel Hill)

P.W. Glidewell.
(Photo courtesy
N.C. Collection,
UNC Library at
Chapel Hill)

Judge Cameron
MacRae, who
presided over
Alma's trial.
(Photo courtesy
N.C. Collection,
UNC Library at
Chapel Hill)

P.W. Glidwell pleading Alma's case in crowded courtroom.
(Photo courtesy N.C. Collection, UNC Library at Chapel Hill)

township, was accepted as the second juror at 11:05, only to be challenged in the afternoon and not allowed to serve, robbing Reidsville of its only member of the jury.

Neither the state nor the defense showed any signs of worrying about how long the jury selection was taking. Both said they were looking for men of intelligence. And both seemed to favor men with large families. Alex Vernon and C. H. Mathews, with twelve and ten children respectively, were selected. But the champion daddy of them all, Y. L. Carter, was ruled out. P. W. Glidewell let him go, even though he knew that Carter didn't like "Pardue preaching." The lawyer knew that although Carter was well informed and had plenty of horse sense, he was too hard-headed for the defense to take a chance on; he just might take any kind of notion about Alma.

As the hardheaded farmer was leaving with the money for his day's work, one of the county officials asked him how many children he had. Mr. Carter seemed disappointed in himself when he answered, "Only fifteen 'yit'."

Attorney Glidewell pointedly asked each prospective juror about his church affiliation; and it was discovered that one-fourth of them had no church membership, though many of them said they attended the Primitive Baptist Church occasionally.

At first, the prosecuting attorney, Porter Graves, had objected strongly to the defense's inquiries about the veniremen's religion, arguing that "church and state are divorced in the laws of North Carolina, and it is immaterial and improper for veniremen to be examined in this manner." But Attorney Glidewell explained that the defense felt that owing to the peculiar circumstances of the case and in view of the state's chief witness being a Baptist minister, they were entitled to question prospective jurors as to their church affiliations as a matter of information for the defense.

Judge MacRae overruled the solicitor's objection, holding that the defense could properly ask the question, and the examination proceeded. Solicitor Graves listened without further comment while the defense asked questions that included: "To what church do you belong?" "Do you know the Reverend Thomas F. Pardue?" "Have any members of your family ever been ministers?" "Have you read the alleged interview by the Reverend Pardue?"

On Wednesday morning at 11:45, the jury was finally completed. A list of the jurymen follows:

J. B. ALBERT, farmer, Huntsville township.
A. S. KNIGHT, farmer, Huntsville township.
T. R. SIMPSON, farmer, New Bethel township.
ALEX VERNON, farmer, Madison township.
A. G. ANGEL, farmer, Huntsville township.
C. H. MATHEWS, farmer, Stoneville.
W. M. CARTER, merchant, Stoneville.
A. J. LEMONS, store clerk, Mayodan.
THOMAS BARKER, farmer, Mayo township.
J. E. CHRISTOPHER, farmer, Huntsville township.
JOHN DANIEL, farmer, Ruffin township.
C. W. ANGEL, farmer, Mayo township.

According to *The Reidsville Review*, the average age of the twelve jurors was 47 years, and they had a total of 48 children. The paper also stated that "four jurors were non-church members, two Methodist Protestant, two Methodist Episcopal, two Christian, one Primitive Baptist, one Missionary Baptist."

The Raleigh News and Observer, which billed itself as "the only daily paper in the world having more subscribers than the population of the city in which published," obviously unaware that the defense had somehow allowed two Baptists to slip through, printed some thoughtful comments on the way the jurors were selected in the Gatlin murder case. The newspaper's editorial follows:

"It seems still to be the fashion to exclude from the jury box as much intelligence as possible. The latest is the challenging of talesmen in the Gatlin murder charge and setting aside all Baptists who are called as possible jurymen. The theory is that because Rev. T. F. Pardue, who reported to officers that Mrs. Gatlin had told him while at a revival meeting that she had killed her father, is a Baptist minister, all Baptists would be inclined to uphold him and be biased against the defendant.

"And this in the year of our Lord 1928! If excluding jurors because they happen to belong to the same church to which a material witness belongs, where will it be possible to secure enough intelligent men to try causes? Moreover, without being so intended, it is a reflection upon the intelligence and fairness of members of that great church to suppose they would be influenced in the slightest because Rev. Mr. Pardue happens to be of that faith. They are Baptists at church and in denominational affairs. Outside the denominational duties, they are citizens. The history and tradition of the independence of church and state among Baptists is proof against their bringing their church affiliations in the jury box."

13

When the Gatlin trial was postponed until the special term of Superior Court beginning February 13, as ordered by Governor Angus W. McLean, this meant that Judge Thomas J. Shaw, sometimes referred to as a "quite just but hard-boiled jurist," would not be presiding. Instead, Judge Cameron F. MacRae, who had the reputation of being equally fair and hard-boiled, would preside over the special term. Although this represented his first visit to Rockingham County in his capacity as a judge, MacRae was no stranger to many people in the county. Before deciding to study law, he was employed for a number of years in the offices of Marshall Fields Corporation in Leaksville.

S. Porter Graves, beginning his twenty-sixth year as solicitor of the same judicial district, had tried more cases than any other solicitor in North Carolina. Recognizing that the Gatlin case promised to be one of the most important trials of his distinguished career, the solicitor from Surry County had announced to the court that because of throat trouble, he had called in Reidsville attorney Will Dalton to assist prosecution.

With Rockingham Solicitor Allen H. Gwyn already serving as his assistant, Solicitor Graves felt most fortunate, since he was well aware that without the intensive investigative work already done by the young attorney, aptly called the man-of-the-hour by one newspaper, he would be ill-prepared to prosecute the case.

P. W. Glidewell explained to the court that although he and Allen Gwyn were partners in a law firm, Attorney Gwyn limited his practice to civil cases. This was something already known by anybody

95

who took the trouble to read the professional business cards that regularly appeared in *The Reidsville Review*. But P. W. thought it wise to clear the air, make it plain that even though the two partners now found themselves on opposite sides of the fence, with Glidewell leading the defense and Gwyn assisting Porter Graves for the prosecution, there was no conflict of interest. Judge MacRae said he was sure that the people in the community understood.

But these calm moments in the courtroom atmosphere were not to last. Tempers would flare, as some already had. Dramatic revelations were to come that would electrify the audience. In other situations, there would be laughter. And occasionally, even Alma Petty Gatlin would find something to smile about.

Many thought the newspapers were exaggerating when they reported that upwards of 10,000 people were crowding into Wentworth every day, hoping to get a seat for the trial. That couldn't be right, the skeptics said; that was more than Reidsville's total population of 8,000 people.

Given the sensational nature of the case, some hyperbole was to be expected, but the reporters may not have been far off in their estimates of the size of the crowds that overran Wentworth.

Located in the center of Rockingham County, Wentworth had been chosen the county seat in the 1780s, and 100 years later the village had about 500 residents and two taverns. By 1928 the gradually dwindling population was variously estimated at anywhere from 100 to 150 people and only Wright Tavern, built in 1816, still remained. Its business had declined drastically since the previous century, when it was a popular gathering place. People had vacationed at the tavern and enjoyed bathing in the mineral springs two miles away; and when court was in session, judges and lawyers stayed at the convenient tavern across the road from the courthouse. But all that had changed and now those who lived in the county returned to their homes at the end of each day's session; others stayed at the Belvedere Hotel in Reidsville.

Every day, automobiles were parked for about half a mile on both sides of the road between Reidsville and Wentworth, and the congestion around the courthouse overflowed toward the west in the direction of Madison. People came from all over the county and from several larger cities about the state, as well. One teacher brought the entire graduating class from nearby Stoneville High School to the trial, only to be turned away from the packed courtroom, which normally could seat no more than 700 people, although some newspapers reported its capacity as 800.

Folding chairs, borrowed from the undertaking parlors of Reidsville, Madison and Leaksville were brought in by resourceful spectators, who added to the congestion by squeezing in extra seats all over the courtroom.

Although court didn't convene until 9:30 each morning, many people would be in the courtroom by 7:00 a.m., ready to spend the day, as evidenced by women with their knitting in their laps. Other people, afraid of not gaining admittance, spent the night in the courthouse.

Paul Jones recalled one day in particular when he and his brother Johnny, 18 and 16 years old respectively, went with their father, R. M. Jones, early enough to get choice seats on the aisle in the middle of the courtroom. But they didn't stay for the trial. Money came hard on the farm they worked on the Narrow Gauge Road, and when three men from Greensboro offered each of them a dollar for his seat, it was too much money for them to turn down.

Large numbers of spectators brought their lunches, packed in brown paper bags, so they wouldn't have to leave their seats. But the judge soon put a stop to the practice of bringing food into the courthouse, after he was told about all the empty pop bottles and paper bags that littered the floor every day.

One morning, the jammed gallery had to be cleared when it was discovered that it had sunk several inches, compounding the problem of people pressed together on the lower stairway. Hemmed in by the crowd, which stood patiently in the aisles during the noon recess of an hour and a half, a young girl fainted, and because everybody was squeezed so close together, the fainting victim literally did not have enough room to fall to the floor. Two men next to her accomplished the seemingly impossible: After much squirming and pushing and pleading, they finally managed to open up a space large enough to get her into an office until she felt better.

Mutt Burton and Jay Swann went one day. It was cold and rainy, and that was bad enough, but fighting the crunch of the crowd and having to stay in their seats all day, for fear of losing them, was worse. It was no place for two young men who made no secret of liking their comforts. They didn't go back.

Outside the courthouse, thousands of people who couldn't get in hunched their shoulders against the rain mixed with sleet. Paying little attention to the man hoping to sell Bibles and dictionaries from the back of his truck, they gravitated toward the sound of music to be entertained by banjo-pickers and comedians on wagons set up by rival medicine men, who touted their remedies as being good for man or beast, guaranteed to cure what ailed you. Traditionally represented as an Indian herbal tonic, the medicine usually consisted of just enough fluid extract of cascara, which indeed was made from a bark, to give a rich brown color to the liquid that contained 40 percent alcohol. At a dollar a bottle, it was over twice as high as comparable patent medicine at the drugstore. But the comedians were funny, the music was entertaining, and the medicine man was a fast-talker with a convincing pitch; so the people bought his colored water with a kick and enjoyed the excitement of being in the crowd, even if they couldn't get into the courthouse where a sensational murder case was unfolding.

After little or no effort was made on behalf of recently executed Ruth Snyder, whose photograph was surreptitiously snapped by a *New York Daily News* reporter just as the current raced through the convicted murderer's body, hurtling her against the electric chair straps, the members of the Massachusetts Society for the Abolishment of Capital Punishment realized they had been dragging their feet.

The Alma Petty Gatlin murder trial was just what they needed to get them back on track. Should this young woman be found guilty and sentenced to die in the electric chair, this powerful organization,

Manton Oliver, right, editor and publisher of *Reidsville Review,* outside the courthouse during a break in the trial. (Photo courtesy N.C. Collection, UNC Library at Chapel Hill)

backed by unlimited cash and an influential membership, promised to send the famous Chicago lawyer, Clarence Darrow, to plead for the commutation of her death sentence.

The trial would not have attracted the interest of a group in New England opposed to the death penalty had it not been for the extensive newspaper coverage that came about because of the ecclesiastical questions raised when a preacher revealed a penitent's alleged confession.

The Associated Press and other wire services were sending out daily reports of the trial in Wentworth. Reporters in town to cover the trial came from Atlanta; Danville, Virginia; Charlotte and other North Carolina towns that included Winston-Salem; Greensboro; Raleigh; Madison; and Leaksville. Also, in the press box every day was journalist Manton Oliver, editor and publisher of the family-owned *Reidsville Review.*

The attention being focused on Reidsville as the scene of the crime and on Wentworth, the site of the trial, brought to mind a quote from a famous friend of Mr. Charlie Penn's.

An executive of The American Tobacco Company with an office in New York, Mr. Charlie liked to get out of the big city on weekends and travel by train to Reidsville. Sometimes, he would invite as his house guest the nationally known humorist and writer, Irvin S. Cobb, a homely man with an exceptional mind.

On a pretty summer's day, the two close friends were said to enjoy good conversation spiked with southern storytelling and mint juleps served on the spacious front lawn of the handsome Penn House on Maple Avenue, while in the large backyard, Miss Teddy's peacocks strutted splendiferously, proclaiming their feathered royalty with strange shrill cries peculiar to the exotic fowls.

When Irvin S. Cobb said that "what North Carolina needed was a press agent," it was meant as a compliment, undoubtedly paid before Alma Petty Gatlin's alleged confession to Rev. Thunderbolt Tom Pardue and the ensuing trial that would put both Wentworth and Reidsville on the map.

But it was not the kind of publicity that either town wanted. And certainly not what Mr. Cobb had in mind for North Carolina, a state he found beautiful, and Reidsville, a town he loved to visit.

14

Several weeks before she went on trial, Alma Petty Gatlin had told reporters, "I want the jury to acquit me or send me to the electric chair. Rather than spend five years in prison, I prefer electrocution."

Lawyer Glidewell would just as soon have had Alma a little less outspoken. But he recognized that she was a strong-willed young woman with definite opinions, and he'd had to smile secretly over a letter he wasn't supposed to know about. Alma allegedly had written to a girlfriend offering the advice that "doing it with men was better for you than masturbation," which was widely believed in those days to be injurious to one's health.

But since becoming Alma's chief attorney, P. W. Glidewell had enjoyed few light moments; he was all but consumed with his determination to defeat the admissibility of Rev. Pardue's testimony.

Attorney Glidewell was quoted as having said, after the trial of Alma Petty Gatlin was over, that the defense team had "tried the preacher." Whether or not he actually made such a statement, it did seem during the course of the trial that "trying the preacher" was the main strategy of Alma's lawyers.

Determined to discredit the evangelist, the defense began by attempting to show that he had exploited Mrs. Gatlin's alleged confession as a publicity stunt to get his name and picture in the papers. Accused of being paid for his interviews in the newspapers, the preacher slowly stroked his black hair combed straight back from his forehead and steadfastly denied that he had received any money. Insisting that he had welcomed the interviews as opportunities to show his side, he explained that it was a matter of conscience with him, and as a citizen of North Carolina and a minister of the gospel, he had done what he was convinced was right.

Under Attorney Glidewell's persistent grilling, Pardue admitted "he had drunk brandy while he was sick" and also said "he had taken a drink of whiskey several years ago before he became an minister of the gospel."

In his grueling cross-examination, Glidewell had directed questions at the preacher that succeeded in making him feel as though he were the one on trial. Tension tightening his mouth, the preacher's lips were compressed to the thinness of a horizontal pencil line, but his black eyes blazed with defiance and he refused to be rattled, taking his time as he answered each question in a mechanical voice. Far from a stupid man, the evangelist knew that the witness box was not the place for the fiery delivery that characterized his animated style when conducting a revival.

Rev. Pardue's reputation as a preacher and a man was at stake, as he had known from the beginning it would be, once he told Alma's story; but as he calmly answered each question, no matter how harshly put, he knew in his heart that he would do the same thing again.

When P. W. Glidewell accused Rev. Pardue of "splitting a church in Leaksville wide open" with his revival in that city, the preacher admitted that he had been challenged by part of the congregation at a Leaksville Baptist church over whether he had been endorsed by Dr. Charles E. Maddry, secretary of the Baptist State Convention. Pardue said that Dr. Maddry had denied that he had endorsed him but later had written him an apology, which he would be glad to offer in evidence.

The words were barely out of the evangelist's mouth when the courtroom exploded with loud handclapping. Judge Cameron MacRae sprang forward in his chair and loudly pounded his gavel, demanding order in the court.

Instantly, Attorney Glidewell jumped to his feet. Livid with rage, he shook his fist toward the cheering section in the rear of the courtroom and shouted, "I defy any of you to try to influence the jury." Determined to be heard, he continued in a loud voice, "Anybody who will applaud while a girl is here on trial for her life, ought not to be allowed to sit in a courtroom with decent people." Still fuming, the lawyer sat down beside Alma.

As the outburst subsided, Alma leaned toward her lawyers and told them that Brother Pardue coached his congregations to deliver their footstompings and handclaps of approval. She said she had helped to applaud on cue many times.

Glidewell immediately rose to his feet, remembering this time to keep his temper in check. He had to be in full control when he went after Pardue about his style and accused him of packing the courtroom to show his strength. Though the preacher declared he "was never more surprised," Alma's chief attorney continued to hammer away at Pardue, trying to force an admission from him that he had orchestrated the demonstration. The preacher denied having anything to do with it, reiterating that he was not expecting it and making the point that he had no way of knowing whether or not his friends took part in it.

Glidewell tried almost everything in his extensive bag of courtroom tricks. But he was unable to rattle Rev. Pardue, who remained calm throughout his attacker's questioning until finally the frustrated lawyer gave up and sat down.

When Judge MacRae had called for a conference between the lawyers, it looked as though the trial might be stopped on the grounds of an attempt to influence the jury. "I am here defending this prisoner and doing the best I can to represent her, and I am doing nothing else," Glidewell said. "And I'm not afraid of that mob out there," he added, turning from the judge and hissing his contempt for the demonstrators, some of whom were shaking their heads while being ordered out of the courtroom by the sheriff's deputies.

The judge, disgusted with the unexpected display of bad manners by the crowd, had been tempted to rule the case a mistrial, but he wanted to be fair to both sides. During the half-hour conference, Glidewell said he didn't ask for any exception and was prepared to proceed. But the crafty, freckled-faced lawyer didn't say whether the defense, if there were a conviction, would take the appeal on the ground of partisan display. He did state, however, that the defense waived no rights. Defense did not object formally to the outburst, but the court took judicial notice of it. The defense had its motion to throw the case out preserved, so when the state rested, defense could still act on the issue at the close of the trial.

Judge MacRae, who had thought about it long and hard before deciding to allow the trial to proceed, was surprised when Attorney Glidewell asked for an adjournment shortly after 4:00 o'clock, explaining that the "heat of the courtroom" had made him very tired.

15

Solicitor S. Porter Graves and Defense Attorney P. W. Glidewell had much in common, including brilliance and cunning, but in other respects they were quite different.

Lean-faced and kindly-looking, Solicitor Graves was a courtly man in his early sixties with a gentle, insinuating voice that "crept into one's ears," as described by one reporter. The moment he stood up to speak, a respectful silence would fall over the courtroom. But the learned rhetorician was frequently guilty of overrefinement of the King's English, with the result that more often than not, the questions he put to the jurymen were over their heads.

P. W. Glidewell, on the other hand, spoke their language. Though the former state senator with rusty-brown hair and a full face generously dotted with pale freckles, could be an eloquent spellbinder, he knew that ordinary people, especially farmers, were comfortable with his colloquialisms. His conversational style held their attention, but did little to allay the uneasiness of the twelve men sitting in the jury box who would rather not be there — an interesting contrast to Alma Petty Gatlin's anticipation of taking the stand. Indeed, one day, after the courtroom had been cleared, she briefly seated herself in the witness box. She had never been in a courtroom until her own trial began, she explained, and she wanted to try the witness chair, just to see how it felt.

Her time in the witness box was coming soon enough. Although they realized it was not a sure thing, most everybody, except the defense, seemed to think that Judge MacRae would rule Rev Pardue's testimony admissible as evidence. And if the preacher's testimony was allowed, Alma would have no choice save to take the stand in her own defense. She would have to convince the jury that the preacher was lying and pray that they believed her version of what happened when her father was murdered.

Both the defense and the state knew that without the testimony of Rev. Pardue, the state would have no case. With so much at stake for both sides, the admissibility of the preacher's testimony was the subject of a hot debate. And since the question of a minister's revelation of a confession had never been legally tested in North Carolina, the Gatlin case was attracting a great deal of interest up and down the Eastern Seaboard.

The state contended that there was no statutory provision giving privilege to confessions made to ministers, such as was accorded to lawyers and doctors. But the defense's contention was that because of the innate decency of the ministry and the provision in the constitution which guaranteed freedom of religious worship, no such provision had ever been needed in the constitution in North Carolina.

On Wednesday, February 15, Rev. Thunderbolt Tom Pardue sat in the witness box and stared straight ahead. He was prepared to tell of Alma Petty Gatlin's alleged confession to him when Glidewell began a savage attack on his motives in revealing a "religious secret" and, as Alma's Chief Defense Attorney, he appealed to the court to protect it.

"It is true that the common law confers no privilege on confessor and penitent as it does on lawyer and client and there is no statute to protect religious confession in North Carolina," Glidewell said. "But the constitution gives this protection and under it this witness should not be allowed to tell of a confession wrung by him from a young woman by holding up the fear of Hell and the hope of Heaven."

At one point, the abrasive lawyer called the clergyman's appearance in court as the chief witness for the state "repulsive, despicable and unheard of."

Before his testimony was challenged as a privileged communication, Rev. Pardue had described how Mrs. Gatlin, moved by the religious fervor of his revival last May, had "opened her heart" to him. After the rest of the congregation had left the warehouse service in Reidsville, the preacher said, Alma told him she had killed her father. And when he asked her how she "got away with it," he said she answered, "It was just like the Snyder-Gray case."

He said she told him she killed her father with an ax, but she didn't say what happened to the body.

The jury was excluded from the courtroom while Attorney Glidewell and Solicitor Graves argued before the judge on the question of the admissibility of the clergyman's testimony.

Glidewell began by asking for the exclusion of Pardue's testimony on the grounds that the alleged confession was not voluntary. "And secondly," he continued, "to admit this testimony in evidence would be to interfere with the constitutional right to worship God according to the dictates of our conscience.

"It would be to interfere with religious liberty. No court, no human authority, has the right to interfere with the inalienable rights of the human conscience.

"Your honor," Glidewell said, looking the bespectacled judge straight in the eye, "this is one of the biggest questions in the courts today. Twenty-two states have passed laws forbidding ministers of the gospel to testify under these circumstances. It is a compliment to the state of North Carolina that the question has never been raised here before. There never has been a necessity for it being called to the attention of the legislative body, because in North Carolina the constitution itself forbids a preacher or priest from revealing a confession.

"Then, your honor, if a minister should tell me that in order to get right with God, I must go to a preacher and confess, and I do that and he goes to tell it to officers, then can I be denied my constitutional rights?

"Can it be possible that a man who claims to be a minister of the gospel can preach 'hell-fire and brimstone,' bring a confession from a penitent, and while she is under the spell, go out and call an officer -- a thing as despicable as that?"

Solicitor Porter Graves quickly countered that the relationship of "the priest and the penitent" was not present in this case. "There is a church which recognizes and practices the confessional," he explained, "but the church to which this man belongs does not subscribe to that doctrine.

"What else was this man to do as a citizen? Was he to bear this burden of knowledge alone in his breast? I can see no reason for this vindictive denunciation of a man who says he is a minister of the Christian religion which is based on the repentance and confession of sins and thereby to seek salvation.

"Then, if a person comes to a minister and confesses

voluntarily to murder, what is the duty of that man as a citizen? Has he to let that knowledge linger to torment him?

"I would suggest, your honor, that in this case there was no evidence that a man whom God had fashioned was missing.

"The priest has the power of absolution of sins, but there was no suggestion of that in this instance.

"When a man has proclaimed God's words of repentance and salvation and someone, not charged with any crime, not under indictment, comes voluntarily to make an admission, what is this man to do?

"That, I suggest, your honor, is a matter entirely for the man to arrange with his conscience and his God.

"I submit then that there is a voluntary admission by a person not under indictment, a statement made to a man who had to decide what was the duty of a citizenship coupled with that of a minister. The law should compel no man to suffer the agony of the ordeal of that knowledge through all the years."

Taking cognizance of how important to both the state and the defense was the question of the admissibility of the preacher's testimony, Judge McRae listened patiently while the two lawyers went on and on for two hours before the seesawing arguments of their verbal tilt came to a standstill. The judge then announced that he would take the matter under advisement and could make no decision before the next morning. Court then adjourned for the day.

In spite of Lawyer Glidewell's protest that Pardue would be violating the confidence of the confessional, Judge MacRae ruled on the following day that the preacher's testimony would be admissible.

The question settled, Pardue resumed the stand and testified that Alma told him that her father, Smith Petty, came home after a year's absence in December, 1926 and began abusing his wife.

The following account highlights the preacher's version of the then unmarried Alma Petty Gatlin's own words when she allegedly confessed to him:

"I interfered in the quarrel and I decided to kill my father. The family all retired except him. He sat up, cursing and playing the phonograph. For two years, I had kept a pistol to kill him with, but I decided to do it with an ax.

"I lay awake waiting for my father to go to bed and to sleep. When I heard him get in bed, I went to the cellar and got the ax. Then I decided if he were found dead in bed, the chances of detection would be too great. I put off killing him until the next morning.

"Mother and sister left the house and father came in for breakfast. I gave him his eggs and went to the kitchen and brought in the ax. Standing behind him, I raised the ax in both hands and brought it down on his head. He fell to the floor and pleaded for mercy while I dealt him two more blows.

"I then dragged him into the kitchen, where I beat him with a pipe. He opened his eyes once and I said, 'Do you believe in Hell now?' He said, 'Yes, pray for me.'"

Pardue testified that Alma said after her father asked her to pray for him, she reminded him that two years before she had told him she would kill him and spit in his face, but she would not spit in his face then.

The preacher continued his testimony. using what he alleged were Alma's own words: "After an hour, he died. I put his body in a trunk and shoved it into a closet. For two days, it stayed there while I dug a grave in the cellar. After all, I decided not to bury it there and took it away from the house in an automobile."

Rev. Pardue went on to say that he had lost ten pounds in the two weeks after Alma made the alleged confession to him. His conscience bothered him fearfully, he said, when he realized the enormity of the crime confessed to him.

The witness said further that he had laid the case before the police of Reidsville, before the prosecutor and before two other lawyers, and none of them would take action.

The preacher didn't see any point in telling the court that just a few days after Smith Petty's body was found last September, he had been present at a three-and-a-half-hour secret session, where he angrily accused police department officials and city manager Joe Womack of being negligent in their duties.

The defense's cross-examination attempted to show that Pardue had cooked up the whole story as a publicity scheme for himself, which seemed highly unlikely to most people in Reidsville, even those who found distasteful the sensationalism often associated with itinerant evangelists.

But who knew what was going through the jurors' minds while Attorney Glidewell was working the preacher over? Their expressionless faces revealed nothing.

The preacher vigorously repudiated newspaper interviews quoting him as saying that he had promised the girl not to divulge her secret if she told him what was preventing her from "getting right with God." He was later to try to smooth over his criticism of the press by saying that he didn't think the newspapers had misquoted him on purpose.

Rev. Pardue remained calm during the cross-examination, while P. W. Glidewell failed to hide his growing impatience with the witness's long answers reiterating his contention that the second confession at his house was solely the result of his desire to save the girl's soul.

The defense produced newspapers quoting the preacher as saying that the girl confessed she had been drunk in a nearby town the night after the alleged confession. Intended to discredit Pardue, the mention of Alma's drunkeness brought a deep blush to her face. And this from the girl who had sat with almost no show of emotion through three days of her trial for patricide.

The preacher's admission that he had made the statement about Alma's being drunk was used by the defense in an attempt to show that publicity for himself, not a feeling of the duties of citizenship, was the motive for his revelations.

It was a grueling cross-examination, but the preacher remained unruffled while Attorney Glidewell charged him with interviewing defense witnesses in an effort to learn their line of testimony. The lawyer sneered at Pardue for driving to Virginia for a special interview with *The Danville Bee* and being paid by the paper. Pardue declared that all the money he had received was two dollars and a half for travel expenses.

The state had scored what seemed a good point when it was brought out from the witness that he had consulted with Attorney P. T. Stiers, now one of Alma's lawyers, before going to the police authorities. But Glidewell shrugged off this information as unimportant, focusing instead on the time it took for Pardue to convince himself that he had to do something about the confession. It was ten or twenty days, the lawyer declared, before he ever gave the girl's name to the police, but he went to see Policeman Buddy Carroll two days after the confession made to the minister in the privacy of his home.

Had Lawyer Glidewell known all the facts, he would have made no mention of Buddy Carroll, for the policeman, at his friend Tom Pardue's suggestion, allegedly was hiding in the closet the night Alma went to the preacher's house on Montgomery Street. Some years later, the policeman confided to a relative that he had heard every word of Alma's confession and she never knew he was in the house.

So why wasn't Officer Carroll introduced as a witness, when he could have corroborated Pardue's testimony that was so vital to the prosecution? Did the preacher ask the officer not to come forward because he was afraid he would appear to be the Judas some of his critics were calling him? This would seem a small price for the preacher to pay for simply trying to establish proof for his assertions. Did somebody pressure Buddy Carroll not to testify? And if this is true, who was it and how did they get by with it?

16

By Friday, with the first week of the trial nearing its end, Alma Petty Gatlin had not yet taken the stand, though it was anticipated that she would testify at the Saturday morning session. And the general feeling was that the trial would continue until at least the middle of the following week. Perhaps longer.

Character witnesses from Yadkin and Forsyth Counties had been heard in defense of Rev. Pardue. The list of witnesses from the western part of the state, where the preacher formerly lived, was impressive and included a former state senator and school teacher, a minister, a doctor, the postmaster of Winston-Salem, and both the sheriff and the clerk of the Superior Court of Yadkin County.

The rest of the day's session was consumed by another string of witnesses called to the stand by the prosecution, beginning with Mrs. John Price, who had occupied the Petty house at the time the body of Smith Petty was exhumed. Nervously twisting a handkerchief in her hand and plainly not enjoying her role as a witness, Mrs. Price testified that Mrs. Smith Petty died on March 9, 1927 and she and her husband moved into the cottage on March 23. She remembered, without giving voice to her thoughts, that she and John had moved in so soon after Alma and the rest left that they were in the house before the Pettys' coal fire in the grate died out.

Mrs. Price then described the house and basement in detail and stated that "she had seen dark spots in the bedroom closet, just over the basement, which had leaked over the coal pile, where the body was found."

She thought about how it had upset her when investigators had come into the house and cut out big pieces of the splotched wallpaper in the dining room and she realized that it must have Smith Petty's blood that had splattered all over the wallpaper. She remembered, too, the straw rug that Alma had left rolled up on the sleeping porch when she moved to Lawsonville Avenue. Mrs. Price had sent the rug to her mother's house on East Market Street, and when it was unrolled and seen to be so dirty and stained, the rug was relegated to the shed out back, where Mrs. Price eventually sent the investigators to check it. She knew now that the dark-brown stains were undoubtedly dried blood and the straw rug must have been in the dining room. But it wasn't up to her to bring all that up; that was up to the people who had done the checking.

The restless witness concluded her testimony by telling the court that one morning when she and Alma were going to church, she said to the defendant, "Alma, I thought I heard a noise around your house (referring to the Petty house, which Mrs. Price was presently occupying) last night. Is your father at home?" The witness said that Alma replied, "No, he wasn't home. You'll never see him up there again."

When Miss Lula Shelton took the stand, she testified that a week after the defendant's mother died, she took an automobile ride to Leaksville with Alma and several other friends. The witness said that Alma became intoxicated and kept murmuring over and over: "It's no use. If you only knew. I can't stand it."

As Miss Shelton stepped down, Alma glared at the girl she thought was her friend.

Another of Alma's so-called friends let her down when Miss Ruth Manley testified that she too had heard Alma's mumblings.

It had been whispered about town for months that Miss Manley's father, who ran a transfer company and taxi service, was the mysterious driver of the Dodge sedan that picked up the trunk after it began leaking blood on the closet floor. The driver's identity was never confirmed, but the gossip persisted. One story making the rounds, accepted by many as the gospel truth, was that Alma and the driver, whoever he was, were going down Lawsonville Road in the middle of the night, heading for Hogan's Creek, where they planned to dump the trunk with the body inside, when they became suspicious of a car behind them. When they would slow down, the other car would slow down. When they would speed up, so would the other car. Convinced it was the police following them, they lost their nerve and went back to the Petty house, with the trunk still leaking blood from the stinking body it contained.

An offshoot of this story was the tale about the driver taking his Dodge to Troy Adams' auto repair shop in Reidsville the next day and requesting replacement of the blood-soaked heavy carpeting that snapped into place on the floorboard in the sedan's back seat. Naturally, Adams would want to know where in the world all that blood had come from. According to the rumor, the man calmly explained that he had hit a dog with his car and in an effort to save the animal's life, he picked up the dog, which unfortunately bled to death in the back of his car before he could get to town.

Next to take the stand was Deputy Dick Stokes, who told the court that in his search for the body of Smith T. Petty, he made a trip to the house the day before and on the day the body was found. He stated that in the course of those two days he made several excavations with the aid of four others before the body was found buried about two feet under the coal pile. He testified that the body was found "face down, with the head doubled-up, and legs that looked as if folded under."

Dr. S. G. Jett told of examining Petty's body, which was "wrapped with a blanket, face downward, with the head under the body and knees drawn, and the flesh about the bones in intervals; had on a suit of underwear; no other garment. One wound on the right side of head two inches above the ear extended five inches from a fracture of the skull. There were other wounds on the left side about the size of a silver dollar."

Charlie W. Jackson, former chief of police, said he viewed the body and identified it. Walter S. Windsor, merchant, and Ed Dix, clerk, also testified that they had viewed the body and identified it as Smith Petty.

Sidney F. Terry, local civil engineer and surveyor who was later to marry Alma's first cousin, Annie Reedy, exhibited blueprints of the house and basement where Smith Petty's body was found.

. . .

The last witness to take the stand before court adjourned until Saturday morning at 9:00 o'clock was John Price, who testified that no work had been done or changes made in the basement during his occupancy of the Petty house. On cross-examination, when asked whether he had employed a plumber to make hot water connections in the house, he said he did, but no digging was done in the basement by the plumber.

The plumber, Henry Webber, was to tell his nephew, Hugh P. Griffin, some years later, that he'd had no idea that he was within a few feet of the body of the murdered man when he was working in the basement. Perhaps it came as an afterthought when he added that he had thought he smelled something funny down there, but didn't think much about it at the time. As it turned out, it gave the plumber something interesting to contribute when a conversation would turn to talk about the Petty Murder Case.

The socially prominent wife of the president of the Bank of Reidsville got a lot of mileage out of her cameo role, unwittingly played in the Petty drama.

Mrs. John F. Watlington, a Yankee transplant with a wonderful sense of humor and a beautiful voice as well, was frequently asked to sing at funerals. Stylish and entertaining, the Pennsylvania native was fond of telling her friends about the time she sang at Mrs. Petty's funeral, which was held in the home, as was the custom in those days. Mrs. Watlington said she had never been more shocked than when she found out later that she had been standing practically on top of Mr. Petty's grave in the basement while she was singing in the living room, where the body of Mrs. Petty lay in its casket.

Many stories have been told about the Petty case, but the one most frequently heard centers on the sighting of buzzards circling the Petty House before the body was found. Of the dozen or so people who told me that they personally saw the buzzards, I don't know how many I convinced of what I believe to be the story's fallacy. I told them I was sure they saw the buzzards all right. But what needed to be cleared up was what really brought the buzzards there.

I don't see how it could possibly have been, as they assumed, the odor of Mr. Petty's body, which was still in its two-foot grave under the coal pile. As one who lived only two doors away and as an eyewitness, as well, to the discovery of the body, I can only say that I certainly did not smell the terrible stench of death and decay until the body was unearthed.

I think the true answer to the mystery of the circling buzzards is to be found when one considers the fact that the Petty house backed up to the holler, where it was not unusual for the kids who played down there to discover among the tangled vines and weeds an occasional dead dog or the body of a cat. To me, it makes sense that it was one or more dead animals that attracted the buzzards to the vicinity. Not Mr. Petty's body.

I'm sure my explanation will never be a popular one, for its acceptance by the people who saw the buzzards would be to rob themselves of a memory perceived as fascinatingly ghoulish and to reduce that memory to the merely ordinary.

I know about that sort of strange fascination, because I share it with a number of people still living who trekked down the hill to see Smith Petty's rotten body, where it lay exposed for four hours before it was removed from the basement.

Because they wish so much that they had seen the body, when in fact they did not, there may be people who have convinced themselves over the years that they did indeed see the murdered man in his shallow grave. And there is certainly no harm in that. But that was not Howard Hardy's style. He had a remarkable memory and was an entertaining storyteller, but he never laid claim to seeing Mr. Petty's body. Though he never said so, I could tell that he wished he hadn't missed his chance.

The way Howard told it, he had just turned 17, was working with a farm family in the rural community of Benaja and couldn't get a ride home until the day after the body was found. As soon as he hugged his mama, he high-tailed it to the Petty house on Lindsey Street, just half a block from where his folks lived on Irvin Street.

Howard was an old man sitting in his regular spot on a bench at the mall when he told me about that day 65 years earlier when he had seen in the trash can near the basement door two dirty rubber gloves, undoubtedly discarded by Dr. Jett after his examination of Smith Petty's remains.

Howard lived to be 88 years old and never forgot the sight of those soiled, smelly rubber gloves and their link to the badly decomposed body seen only in his imagination.

In 1949, the year they were married, Grace Vernon's new husband, Robert Jeffreys, took her by the Petty house, where the Jeffreys family had lived some years after the murder. He wanted to show her something. And there it was, still sitting there: Hugging the hill which sloped from the back of the house toward the holler was a ruined old trunk. Its once hard, rectangular shape softened by years of exposure to the elements, the dilapidated trunk had somehow defied total collapse.

As the young couple stood looking at the trunk, Robert told his wife that people said it was the same one in which Mr. Petty's body had been hidden twenty-two years earlier. Robert said he never could find any good reason to doubt what he'd been told.

I like to believe that the crumbling old trunk near the bottom of the hill that Grace and Robert saw that day over fifty years ago was an authentic relic from a gruesome murder.

17

As a witness for the state, Miss Mary East, a trained nurse who had attended Mrs. Smith Petty in her final illness testified on Friday that the defendant made vague admissions to her during her stay in the Petty home and that she had suspected something was terribly wrong.

In his cross-examination, P. W. Glidewell caught the witness off guard with his opening question. "Miss East," he said, "did you at any time while you were in the Petty home observe this defendant come into her mother's room, fall down on her knees beside the bed, take her mother's hand in hers and beg her to confess?"

The nurse hesitated, bit her lip and looked confused. Mr. Glidewell pressed her.

"She knelt down by her mother's bed and took her hand," admitted Miss East.

"Did she urge her mother to confess?"

"I didn't hear her."

"Were you in the room all of the time?"

"I went to the kitchen to fill hot water bottles."

"Did you hear her tell her mother she was going to die?"

"Yes, she said she was going to die."

"Did you see her when she went away and brought back a minister?"

"She brought a preacher there."

"Did her mother say anything more?"

"No, she went into a coma and never roused any more."

"Did the preacher wait, hoping that she would rouse up?"

"He waited around a while, but was not there when she died," the nurse said.

Solicitor Graves had heard enough. Jumping to his feet, he vigorously protested against the admission of such evidence. "It is self-serving and without standing under the rules of evidence," he contended.

Judge Cameron MacRae, having instructed the jury to leave the room while the point was argued, ruled the evidence out. But P. W. Glidewell had shown his hand: Defense planned to save Alma from the electric chair by proving with her own testimony when she took the stand the next day that it wasn't Alma who had struck the fatal blow; it was her mother who had killed Smith T. Petty.

Although on Saturday the Penn's chauffeur, Pink Cummings, had pointed the big Lincoln toward Wentworth, the destination of his passengers was not the county courthouse. Miss Teddy Penn and Miss Minnie Burton were more interested in doing good works than in hearing Alma's testimony; and their mission that day was to deliver two large baskets of sandwiches to the County Home, often called the poorhouse, a name neither of the Baptist ladies liked, feeling it shamed the people who had nowhere else to go.

About a mile and a half down the road from the County Home, where harmless Crazy Ella lived with aged indigent residents, traffic was congested around the courthouse, and among the several hundred cars parked all about, automobile tags from a dozen North Carolina towns were in evidence, attesting to a statewide interest in the trial.

Deputy Sheriff James H. Pritchett, who was responsible for getting Alma back and forth each day, had safely conducted the prisoner across the road and through the narrow aisle formed outside by hundreds of people unable to gain admittance who lined both sides of the way from the jail to the courthouse.

Progress was slow as the lawman pushed their way up the crowded steps that led to the jammed courtroom on the second floor. Once they were inside the courtroom, the relieved deputy turned Alma over to Sheriff Chunk Smith who escorted the prisoner to her usual seat at the table with her lawyers.

The night before, the prisoner had gone to sleep early, before the jail lights were extinguished, and awakened cheerful — singing and smiling, her optimism undoubtedly boosted by the hundreds of communications expressing sympathy which had poured in from all parts of the country during her incarceration.

Her chief attorney, P. W. Glidewell, had been encouraged and pleased by letters he received while the trial was in progress from three Catholic nuns in New York who wrote that it was their belief that Rev. Pardue had violated a sacred trust by revealing a penitent's confession and they were praying for Alma's deliverance.

Dressed in a tan suit, Alma Petty Gatlin presented a perfect picture of poise that Saturday morning when she took the oath and mounted the stand at 9:12.

Glidewell had obviously prepared his client well, for Alma appeared confident and the tilt of her retrousse nose seemed to set off her defiance of Solicitor Porter Graves, known and respected as a tough prosecutor who had already sent one white woman to death row in Raleigh.

Solicitor Graves had surprised the court when he announced his decision to invite Rev. Pardue to sit behind the prosecution and prompt them while Alma testified. The preacher's presence with the prosecution, considered by many a master stroke for the state, added to the drama of the one hour it would take the defendant to give her testimony. An hour during which the preacher would rarely take his eyes off the girl on trial for her life. But Alma's expression, when she returned his stare, would register only disdain. And during her testimony, she was to look into the jury's eyes and, speaking across the attorneys' table to where Pardue sat, she would charge him with betraying her trust after she had bared her soul to him and accuse him of lying. Yet this complex woman would later credit the preacher with a general desire to tell the truth.

Alma began her testimony by stating in a clear voice that she had lived in Reidsville "about eight years, the best I remember," adding that she had lived in Hanes, North Carolina before moving to Reidsville.

"Who composed your family, Mrs. Gatlin?" Glidewell asked.

"My mother, my father, my sister Thelma and two brothers, Woodrow and Smith, Junior, my cousin Annie Reedy and myself."

"How long had you lived in this house on Lindsey Street?"

"Mr. Glidewell, I don't remember; it was over a year, though. I think."

Alma Petty, left, in the Candy Kitchen, where she
worked as a teenager for Pete and Neely Sacrinty.
(Photo courtesy the late Fred Ballenger)

The witness stated that she was twenty-one years old last
August the 30th and she had been working about four years altogether,
she thought.

When asked what kind of work she had been doing, Alma
answered that for two years she had worked for Pete and Neely Sacrinty
in a soda shop called the Candy Kitchen. "And I had been with Dr.
Meador as his dental assistant for about eighteen months, I believe."

She didn't mention her first regular job: selling tickets at the
Grand Theatre, where she had met her future husband, the theatre's
film projectionist.

Alma continued her testimony, stating that her mother had

122

been working since they had been in Reidsville. "About — I believe a little over six years," Alma said and explained that Mrs. Petty worked for Mrs. Cornie Irvin at her ladies apparel store for about a year, and then she went to work as a clerk at Belk-Stevens Department Store the day that they opened.

Alma said her father had lost out at the mill in Reidsville about five years ago and since then he had worked at various cotton mills out of town. He would show up at home right out of the blue and the next thing they knew he would be gone again to wherever he heard a good cotton mill man could find work, and the family rarely knew his whereabouts.

Her two younger brothers were still in school, she said, and didn't work.

P. W. Glidewell then asked Alma to describe how the rooms were located in the house she lived in on Lindsey Street.

Alma said, "It was a five-room house and had one hall and a sleeping porch. On the left side of the house, as you entered, there were four rooms - living room, bedroom, dining room and kitchen. On the right side of the door as you entered, there was one bedroom and the bath, and straight through the front hall there was this sleeping porch used as a bedroom."

"Describe the basement," Glidewell said.

"It had four rooms, I think: one room directly under the living room, and there was a large room next to the first room and it covered

Alma's siblings, left to right, Thelma, Woodrow, and Smith, Jr. (Photo courtesy N.C. Collection, UNC Library at Chapel Hill)

the dining room and part of the kitchen, and then there was a small room that was under part of the kitchen, and on the right side of the basement there was a large room."

"Was there a stairway that led down to the basement?"

"Yes, sir, it led down from the back porch; it was directly outside the kitchen, down to another porch on the ground floor."

"Mrs. Gatlin," Glidewell said, pausing briefly before abruptly changing his line of questioning, "when was your father killed?"

The witness fixed the time her father was killed at about eight o'clock on the morning of January 10th, 1927, stating that he had come home unexpectedly the night before, after a long absence.

When Alma was asked by Glidewell to tell the jury in her own way just what happened the night before her father was killed and what happened the next morning, her mood started to change and she gradually began to increase the tempo of her testimony. The more the drama heightened, the faster she talked. And several times later in her testimony, she was to break into wild sobs but would quickly recover and rush on with her story.

Alma said that she, her sister and their cousin had gone to church on Sunday night, January 9th, and when they left church it was snowing. She said that when they got home and were in the front hall taking off their coats, they heard Mrs. Petty scream. The defendant ran into the room and saw her father choking and beating her mother as she lay on her bed, where she had spent most of the day suffering from a nervous headache.

"I hollered not to do her that way," Alma said. "And Father said, 'What in the hell have you got to do with it?' and slapped Mother in the face again."

Solicitor Graves objected, saying that what occurred on the previous day could have no bearing on the homicide. Objection was overruled.

"My sister and cousin had hurried into the room right behind me," Alma continued, "and they helped me pull him away from her bed. He picked up a stool and started back toward her bed, and said he was going to burst her head wide open. When I tried to grab the stool, he knocked me unconscious and I fell to the floor.

"When I came to, I heard my sister and cousin begging Mother to let them go for an officer to protect us. Father dared us to do it, saying if we did, it would be like another Carter-Moore affair, but he'd do better than Austin Carter — he'd kill the whole bunch."

. . .

The mention of the "Carter-Moore affair" referred to the murder of Mrs. John Price's sister, killed in cold blood several years earlier in the home of her parents, Mr. and Mrs. L. L. Moore. Her estranged husband, Austin Carter, a Danville, Virginia, insurance man, shot his wife in the East Market Street residence. Miss Sudie's husband, John Price, was also wounded in the shooting.

Austin Carter had been sentenced to die in the electric chair, but the day before his scheduled execution, the governor commuted the sentence to life imprisonment.

Alma continued her testimony, stating that her father left the house cursing and vowing he would return that night and kill them all. After he was gone, they tried to persuade their mother to let them get an officer, but she wouldn't allow it, declaring she would rather die, would rather anything happen than to go through the disgrace of airing the family's dirty linen.

That night, about 12 o'clock, her father returned to the house, Alma said. He cut all the lights on and began kicking things over in the front hall and all over the house. They asked him not to burn the lights, which the women had to pay for. His response was to go to the basement and stay down there thirty or forty minutes, kicking a tin bucket on the floor and knocking on the ceiling under her mother's bedroom and the living room, so the family could not sleep. Finally, he came up the stairs with a bucket of coal. He set the coal bucket down and cut on the lights in the bedroom. He was carrying an "iron stick" and held a butcher knife in his right hand. Her mother begged him to put up those things and cut out the light and go to bed. He wouldn't cut the light out and said he needed the light to do what he meant to do. He'd been waiting all these years for a chance to kill them all, he said.

"'There won't be anybody left here in this family but me,' he said, 'and it don't make any difference anyhow.'

"I had just got back in bed when Father came in cursing because I'd turned the light out. He was insanely drunk and began shaking the bed. Then he resumed his attack on Mother, slapping her and throwing a dish from the bureau, which hit her in the stomach. She screamed and my sister and brother and cousin came running into the room. He threw a brush at them and cursed them, and wanted to know what in the hell they wanted in there. It took all of us to get him out of there and into the living room. He was still acting like a crazy man. He played the victrola for an hour and a half and didn't go to bed until about four o'clock in the morning. But he was up again by five-thirty, or about that time.

"Next morning, my mother called the oldest boy, about six o'clock, to make the fire in her room, which he always did; and when the fire was built, he called my sister and my cousin to fix breakfast about six-thirty. About seven o'clock, or a little after, they called us to breakfast and my mother and I got up and put on our kimonos and went in to breakfast. Annie Reedy, or Thelma one, went to call my father, who was in the living room. He came into the dining room and said he didn't want any breakfast and it wouldn't do us any good to eat any.

"My mother and my sister and my cousin and the youngest brother and I all sat down at the table and had breakfast together. Woodrow, my oldest brother, had been lying down across the foot of my mother's bed, so when he came in to breakfast, I sat with him until he got through. About twenty minutes to eight, he went down in the basement to get up the coal and kindling. Ten minutes later, Thelma and Annie and Smith, Junior, my baby brother, left the house."

"Where was your baby brother going?" Glidewell asked.

"He left there to go to school. I reckon he went."

"Where were your sister Thelma and your cousin Annie going?"

"They were going to Danville to take a note. Must I say why they were going?"

Glidewell answered that she did not have to say, and Alma stated without further elaboration that they were going to Danville to see a doctor.

"Just a few minutes after they left the house — I don't remember, I suppose about eight o'clock," Alma said, "I was bathing my face and washing my neck and ears at the kitchen sink, getting ready to go to work, when I heard my father walking through the sleeping porch and into the dining room; but I thought he was coming to breakfast. I thought he would be kind of sobered up by then, and I didn't think he would be dangerous."

She said her father appeared in the doorway that led from the dining room to the kitchen and snarled, "You needn't be washing your damned neck. I'm going to cut it off — now!" Then he drew back a big butcher knife to show he meant business and sailed into her.

The witness, talking faster and faster, seemed on the verge of hysteria and had to be calmed down by Lawyer Glidewell, who asked her to talk more slowly, so her testimony could be understood.

Alma regained control of herself and related how she tried to keep her father from cutting her throat and had caught her father's wrist with her right hand. He dropped the knife and started choking her. She pulled free and grappled with him, screaming as loud as she could.

"What would have happened, I don't know," she said. "My mother rushed in through the dining room door and screamed, 'Smith, don't hurt Alma; turn her loose! She is not the cause of this. She can't help it if I didn't get rid of it.' At about the same time, my brother Woodrow came running through the kitchen door leading from the back porch. My brother had the ax in his hand and ran toward us with it upraised. My mother seized the ax from his hands and struck my father in the back of the head.

"Whether the blow whirled us around or whether it was my father jerked me around, I don't know, but he fell and my knees were sinking. He was still holding to my throat. I had his hands and I was trying with my left hand to get his left hand off my throat and he fell up against the wall. I fell under him with my knees pressed against him and my mother was still screaming not to hurt Alma, she was not the cause of this, and his hold did not relax the least bit. She raised the ax again and struck him somewhere about the face. My father's grip on me relaxed and he took a step or two forward and tripped me backwards as he fell to the floor and I fell across him. I was stunned a little from hitting the back of my head on the floor when I fell and Mother helped me get up. My father didn't move and we knew he was dead.

"We left him lying there and went out of the kitchen into the dining room. I remember seeing Mama take her foot and close the kitchen door and we went into her room. We were all scared and crying and didn't know whether or not to call the police. But Mother said, 'No, we won't tell the police or anybody else. I have always kept things secret and I'll not start letting them out now. I'd rather wait and get myself together before deciding what to do.'

"I begged her to send after the chief of police, to send my little brother next door to the Mitchells — we didn't have a telephone — and call for the officers; there was not anything the law could do, everything was right there to show just how it happened. But she said no, she would die, she would kill herself before our very eyes; we would not have just one death in the family, there would be two; that she would kill herself if it ever got out in any way. She couldn't face the disgrace, she said. She made me finish dressing and insisted that I — or demanded that I go to work and my brother go to school; and that would leave her alone there with my father. I was afraid she would kill herself, she was as nervous and scared to death as I was. We made her promise if we did leave she would not harm herself. She swore she would not kill herself and followed us to the front door, warning us not to let the other children know what had happened, and told us if she was there when we got home to promise not to say anything to the officers and not to worry if she wasn't there and did not come back for several days. We left and my brother Woodrow walked part of the way to Doctor Meador's office with me, as far as the Belvedere Hotel, and I suppose he went to school; he left me to go to school."

The witness said when she got home from work between 5:30 and 6 o'clock and found her mother in bed, she thought at first that she had taken poison. Alma's baby brother was in the room sitting before the fire and she asked him to leave because she wanted to know what had happened. He went into the kitchen where Thelma and Annie Reedy were fixing supper and Alma sat down on her mother's bed and noticed she had been crying. Her mother refused to answer questions about what had happened and said she didn't want Alma or Woodrow, either one, to ask her what had been done with the body. All her mother would say was everything is all right. "Alma, you have seen too much, your life is ruined now; don't ask me any more," she quoted her mother's saying.

But Alma persisted in questioning her mother, insisting she had a right to know what had been done with her father's body. "Finally, Mother told me the body of my father was sent off in a box looking like a trunk and that a Dodge sedan had called for it. But she never told me the name of the man who drove the car."

A tear trickling down her cheek, Alma quietly stated that her mother had died two months later on March 9, 1927. "Doctor Cummings was our regular doctor, but Doctor Abernethy was called in once or twice. Doctor Cummings was the one she wanted when she was taken ill at work Friday afternoon, and I took her home and called him that night. He stayed with her all night and didn't leave until the next morning about four or five o'clock.

"Mother had had a miscarriage and the doctor told me Monday night that there was no chance for her to survive, pneumonia having set in on both sides." Alma said she was afraid her mother was going to die with the secret in her breast and repeatedly asked the doctor if there was no hope. He shook his head and said that he was keeping her alive with heart stimulants and that she might not live through the night.

As the witness described her mother's death room, her sister Thelma, who had been with her in court every day, wept softly.

"I told Doctor Cummings there was something my mother had to tell and I asked if I could send for a minister. He said that I could. I then went back to Mother and found her in labored breathing. I asked Miss East, the trained nurse we had with her, to leave the room for a few minutes. I knelt beside my mother's bed and begged her to tell, not to die with the secret in her heart. She said she'd never tell it and asked the nurse to keep me out of her room. But Wednesday night before she died at eleven-thirty, Mother sent for me and asked me to get a minister so she could make a confession. I asked Mrs. Pearl Leath, my Sunday school teacher, to go get the minister."

The minister, who was never put on the stand, was Rev. H. B. Worley and he lived on the northeast corner of Morehead and Franklin Streets, just a block away from the Petty house. And in the fall of 1927, after the body had been discovered and the newspapers were all featuring stories about the murder, it was an unusual weekend when no strangers from out of town came knocking on the preacher's front door, asking if they could see the hole where the body had been buried in the basement of what they took to be the Petty house. It got so everybody in the Worley household would explain in almost the same words, as if by rote, that they had the wrong corner and they would then direct them to the northeast corner of Lindsey and Franklin Streets.

Alma testified that the minister came at 8 o'clock and she asked him if he believed in deathbed repentance. "He said 'yes' and began quoting the Scripture," Alma said. "Then he went into Mother's room and I begged him to be patient with my mother. I stayed out in the hall while he was in her room. He was in there about twenty minutes; and when he came out, he put his hand on my shoulder and said, 'Alma, your mother recognized me a few times, but she would be unconscious every minute or two. She didn't tell me anything, but I'll wait. She does have something to tell me, I think. I'll wait until she gets better.'"

The state's objection to this evidence, unless the minister was in the courtroom, was sustained.

Alma said her mother never regained consciousness again and died that night at about 11:30.

Dr. M. P. Cummings corroborated Alma's testimony of her efforts to get a confession from her mother. The doctor said, "Alma told her mother that she must not leave us all here; we can't stand it."

In her testimony, Alma admitted visiting the house on Lindsey Street three times after she moved to Lawsonville Avenue, but she denied ever going into the basement. But the story told later by Gene Smith suggests that she did go into the basement after she no longer lived in the house where Gene rented the front bedroom from Mrs. Sudie Price.

Gene was a wanderer, a small man with itchy feet, who never stayed in one place very long. And he had already moved, as far away as Timbuktu for all anybody knew, when the short-lived rumor began to circulate that the body found in the basement in September was the man who'd had a room at the Petty house that summer.

Gene had been awakened late one hot July night by a loud knocking on the outside door to his bedroom and there on the front porch stood Alma and Eugene Gatlin with Mary Lewis Kemp and Self Davis. Alma told Gene Smith that the two couples had just gotten married and she persuaded him to give up his bedroom for that one night.

Recalling a chance remark Miss Sudie had made, Alma knew the Prices wouldn't be there. Since John Price was staying overnight with a farmer friend whom he was helping thresh wheat, his wife had chosen to spend the night at her mother's house. So one couple used the Prices' bedroom and the other pair occupied Gene Smith's room. Though Gene never did say where he slept, he probably spent the rest of the night on the sleeping porch floor, since the bed Woodrow formerly shared with his daddy when he was home was no longer back there.

The next morning, Alma allegedly went down into the basement to inspect the painting that Bob Corum and Paul Durham had been hired to do, saying she wanted to see if they were doing a good job, and when she came back upstairs she said it looked all right.

Alma's testimony continued as Lawyer Glidewell led the witness, asking her about the Leaksville trip. Alma said that state witnesses Lula Shelton and Ruth Manley had misinterpreted what she meant, that what she had reference to was her mother's secret.

"Tell the jury what you said, if you recall," Glidewell instructed Alma.

"I began crying when the subject of my mother came up about how she died and something was said about they knew that my mother had never done anything wrong."

"Objection," said Solicitor Graves, "unless Miss Shelton said it."

"Miss Shelton was along, but I don't say she said it. But somebody in the party did."

"If it is part of the conversation that Miss Shelton participated in and Miss Shelton heard it, I don't object," said the solicitor.

"Miss Shelton was along; some of the girls began to cry, trying to comfort me, saying that I need not worry, that my mother was always a perfect woman; even if she was not an active church worker, that they didn't think I had anything to worry about. And I did say, 'You don't know, you just don't know. You don't understand like I do; there's something you don't know about.' And I did quote some Scripture. And I did say I didn't believe I could stand it any longer. Yes, sir, I said that."

"Were you drinking that night?" asked Glidewell.

"No, sir, I was not. If there was a soul had a drop, I didn't know it."

"Did you make the statement to Miss East that she testified to, that you had something to tell her when you knew her better?"

"I won't deny that, but I don't remember. I was really disturbed, worried sick about my mother. I was just crazy," she said. Then, turning quickly to the jury, she smiled and said, "But I am not pleading insanity, gentlemen."

Solicitor Graves voiced his objection to the witness' impropriety in speaking directly to the jury. But Judge MacRae, deeming Alma's aside as nothing more than a harmless, albeit improper, attempt at levity, saw no need for comment from the bench.

Lawyer Glidewell glanced toward the judge, who seemed to be waiting for the testimony to continue, then he asked Alma if she was in about the same state of mind she had just described when she made the trip to Leaksville. Her answer was yes, she was still very much worried over the condition under which her mother had died.

"Mrs. Gatlin, did you make the statement that Miss Manley testified to yesterday about if she knew what you knew - I don't remember the exact words she used; do you recall whether that conversation took place?"

"No, sir, I don't remember that. I don't deny it, though; I just don't remember it."

"When you went downtown the day your father was killed, did you go to Doctor Meador's office?"

"Yes, sir."

"What was the condition of your neck, with reference to its being scratched or lacerated?"

"I had not noticed my neck until Doctor Meador came in and he asked me as quick as he came in what was the trouble with my neck. I was still so scared, didn't anything hurt me and I didn't know what he was talking about. I knew I had been choked, but I didn't know there was anything on my neck; and I took a little hand mirror and there was blood on my neck and several long scratches and dents that had been punctured through the skin; and I told Doctor Meador that the baby, Smith, Junior, had brought in a stray cat and I had been playing with it and I got the worst end of the bargain; it scratched my neck."

"Did Doctor Meador treat it by the application of any antiseptic?"

"Doctor Meador painted it with mercurochrome, the back of my neck, and I painted the front of my neck."

"Now, Mrs. Gatlin," Mr. Glidewell said, "I want you to go ahead in your own way and tell about your interview with Mister Pardue; just how it began and under what circumstances and what was said."

As Alma began to speak, the throng of people massed together in the courtroom hung on her every word, listening with a quietness bordering on reverence.

Rev. Pardue's version of her confession, as he had related it on the witness stand, contained a number of discrepancies, she said, and it was time now for the true story to be told, the way she had told it to him.

"It was soon after Mother's Day and I was still worried to

death about the way my mother had died, trying to confess, with the desire to confess, but she had failed. I don't remember the exact date, but it was in May and I went to Mister Pardue's meeting at Pinnix Warehouse. I waited until the congregation was dismissed and everybody was gone, and I went up to the rostrum. Mister Pardue had his coat on his arm and hat in his hand and he was about to leave. I asked to speak to him and we went into the choir loft."

Pardue had preached that night on the "confession of sins," which Alma said magnified her anxiety about her mother's fate. She just had to have an answer. So, trying to hide her nervousness, she said, "I understood you to say that unless a person confessed their sins before death there is no hope for them."

"Yes, that's right," she quoted the minister as replying.

"'Is there only one unpardonable sin?' I asked him.

"'Yes,' he answered, 'a sin against the Holy Ghost.'"

She asked what he meant by that and he said, "Blasphemy of God's children."

She said she then asked the preacher if a murderer could enter the Kingdom of Heaven?

"He glanced at me sharply," she said, "and asked: 'Alma, why are you interested in murder? You have not committed murder, have you?'" She said she did not answer his question.

"I knew what I wanted to ask him, but didn't know how to say it, because I wanted to protect my mother. I could not bear to think of her burning in Hell because she had not been able to confess, though she had wanted to. I decided then and there to take this thing on myself and say that I was guilty of murder.

"He said, 'Alma, you know you didn't commit any murder.'"

"I said, 'Yes, Mr. Pardue, I murdered my father.'"

"He swore with a Bible over his heart that he would not divulge my statement and would keep everything between us and his God.

"I then asked Mr. Pardue if confession was made on the deathbed and if a person who desired to confess a crime had become unconscious before being able to do so — was there any hope for them? I was still thinking of my mother.

"He said, yes, there was hope for them because they had desired to confess. I thanked him and left."

She said that the next day the preacher came to Dr. J. R. Meador's dental office, where she was employed, and questioned her, but she told him she was satisfied with his answer of the night before.

He then left but returned the next day and invited Alma and her friend Blanche Moore to his home to take supper with him and his family and attend the service afterwards.

Alma said when she went by her friend's house the next day, she found Blanche in a housedress, busy helping her mother with the housework. Blanche said it would take her about an hour to finish what she was doing and to dress, and she was afraid it would cause the supper at the Pardue home to be late and cause Mr. Pardue to be late for his services that night. She asked Alma to go on and make apologies for her. So Alma went by herself to the minister's home across the street from the First Christian Church on Montgomery Street, and after supper he sent his children from the room, locked the door, pulled up a chair to her and questioned her.

She said he told her he could not imagine how she could commit such a crime and nobody find out about it. Then he asked her if she had confidence in him; and she said that she told him she had more confidence in him than in any living human being since her mother died.

"He told me he appreciated my confidence and if I had confidence enough to tell him what I did at the warehouse, I ought to have confidence enough to tell him the details.

"He again swore that he would keep anything I told him secret. I did not know how to talk without mentioning my mother," said the defendant, "so I just stuck to my story.

"He asked me whether my father had been shot. I told him my father had been struck with an ax and related much the same details he said here on the stand."

Lawyer Glidewell then asked the witness to relate what had precipitated the violent anger directed at her mother by her father the night before the killing.

"Shall I tell that to the jury?" Alma asked.

"Yes, go right ahead," her attorney replied.

"Well — my mother was pregnant. My father had told her to get rid of it, and he said he wanted no more little brats around the house." Alma said that he told her mother he would kill her if she didn't get rid of it. The witness also mentioned that some years previously her father had gone to Winston-Salem and got some medicine for her mother that would induce abortion.

Alma's testimony sounded to many like a cleaned-up version

of a rumor making the rounds that what had really started all the trouble was Mr. Petty's coming home after a long absence and finding his wife pregnant by another man.

The busybodies were quick to identify the guilty party as a man who roomed at a neighbor's house within walking distance of the drugstore where he worked. The funny part was that the man had been dating Mrs. Petty's pretty daughter Thelma, but when the mama got pregnant the man left town, supposedly returning to Virginia.

Leading the witness back to her account of the conversation at the preacher's home, Glidewell asked Alma to relate what she had told Mr. Pardue about the body.

"He asked what had become of the body of my father, if the officers were not called in and he asked why the officers were not called in and I told him that my mother said she would kill herself before our very eyes if this ever became known. Then he said, 'Why, Alma, I thought you told me you were the only one that knew about this,' and then I had to — "

"What did you tell Mister Pardue about the disposition of the body?"

"I didn't know what to tell him; I didn't know what had become of the body. I had to tell him the truth, all I knew."

"What did you tell him?"

"I told him that the body was taken away in a box about the size of a trunk in a Dodge sedan."

"Is that what your mother had told you?"

"Yes, sir."

"Did you tell Mister Pardue that you had carried a pistol for two years to kill your father?"

"No, sir, I did not. But a pistol was mentioned. When Mister Pardue asked me to describe what kind of man my father was, I told him that he had carried a pistol. It was a pistol he had borrowed from a man down about the Edna Cotton Mill and he carried it for two years. He told us he was just waiting for the right time when he thought he could kill us all and get by with it. I also told Mister Pardue that my father finally lost it when this man met him on the street and beat him up because he would not return his pistol to him; he kept it so long."

"At the conclusion of your conversation at Mister Pardue's house, what happened? Did he pray?"

"Yes, sir, after I told him what I have told you gentlemen, we got up to leave the room and he said, 'Wait a minute, I want to pray with you about this matter.' So we knelt down and he prayed, thanking God for making him such a leader of God's people that a person would have so much confidence in him that they would tell him such a horrible thing as this. And he prayed that God would help him keep the secret as well as the confidence of the people."

"Did he tell you that night or any other time that he was going to report this to the officers?"

"I didn't have the slightest hint in the world it was going before the officers until, I believe it was August the thirty-first, Mister Gwyn asked me to come down to his office; and that was the first time I had any idea that anything was going around, that Mister Pardue had been to the officers. He never gave me any hint."

"Did he beg you to go and confess to the officers?"

"There was not one word suggested about the officers; not one," she said emphatically, as she concluded her testimony.

It had taken Alma only a little more than an hour to relate all the details, most of which caught by surprise the men and women in the courtroom who all these months had found no reason to doubt the newspaper accounts of Rev. Pardue's version of Alma's confession, just as they had found no reason to question the truthfulness of the preacher's testimony earlier in the week.

Now they didn't know who to believe.

18

It was ten-thirty when S. Porter Graves approached the witness box to begin the state's cross-examination of Alma Petty Gatlin. His first question was why Alma had endured over five months in jail when all she had to do was make the statement that her mother had done the killing.

Alma's spirited answer was that she had kept quiet and told no one except her attorneys, because she knew after learning that the preacher had given her away, he had the advantage over her and people would be more likely to believe him than they would her. "I knew that there would have to be a trial about this thing and I decided to keep it all until that time."

Graves dismissed her reply with a mere nod and a barely audible "uh-huh."

The long, angular solicitor's courtroom persona had many facets and he was to exhibit all of them before his questioning of the defendant would be concluded in an hour and twenty-five minutes.

He could, and would, swing from tenderness to sarcasm. Elaborately expansive and soft-spoken, Solicitor Graves was noted for his cleverness in leading an unsuspecting witness into a trap and then he would make a triumphant show of springing the trap. Forewarned by her attorneys of the prosecutor's craftiness, Alma meant to be a wary prey. So while admitting that during her life she had told lots of things that were not true, she let Graves know that now she was up there on the stand to tell the truth and that was what she intended to do.

But it was evident from the beginning that Alma was no real

match for the seasoned solicitor, and within a few minutes he had the defendant contradicting herself, which he verified by reading aloud to the court Alma's own words from her earlier testimony.

The witness denied sending a telegram on March 10 to her father in Franklinton notifying him that her mother had died the previous night. But she said she wrote the message and finally admitted that Eugene Gatlin, who subsequently married her, took it to the telegraph office. She stated that she wrote it because Mr. and Mrs. Ben Setliff brought to her a man who insisted that she telegraph her father. She admitted that she knew Smith Petty would never receive the telegram, since she knew at the time that her father was dead. She justified her actions by saying she was doing all she could to keep down suspicions.

Feeling she had satisfactorily dealt with the issue, she smiled at Mr. Graves and told him that if he had any more of those messages, she would admit sending them, too.

The witness stated that she did not get John G. Scott, superintendent of Edna Cotton Mill, to advertise in the *Textile Bulletin* to find her father. She said the advertisements were inserted by Scott on his own.

The Setliffs and Scott were later to be called by the defense as corroborating witnesses.

Solicitor Graves succeeded in obtaining Alma's admission that she had concealed her knowledge of her father's death, and she further admitted that she had told her husband that she knew nothing about it when he questioned her after hearing rumors several weeks before the investigation began. She also declared that she did not feel uneasy about telling a lie and pretending she was guilty when talking to Rev. Pardue, because she felt justified since she was seeking information about her mother's soul.

At the start of the cross-examination, both solicitor and defendant had seemed to go out of their way to treat each other with almost exaggerated civility. Graves handled Alma with a consideration approaching tenderness, while she politely answered his questions with a respectful "yes, sir" or "no, sir." But the solicitor changed his tone when he sought to shame her for leaving her distraught mother alone with the corpse of her father on the day of the killing. "You went off with your mother in that desperate frame of mind?" he said.

"I was in just as desperate a frame of mind as my mother," Alma retorted.

. . .

The story that Alma had told in her testimony didn't jibe with Pardue's version of her alleged confession and Solicitor Graves, questioning the discrepancies, extended his left hand and pointed a long, bony finger at the defendant as he asked sternly: "Do you deny that you said that?"

Alma smiled saccharinely, first at the solicitor, then at Rev. Pardue, from whom she borrowed her answer. "On the ground that I have no recollection of having said it, I deny it," she said, sweet as pie.

The preacher had used those exact words twenty times in his testimony to escape the relentless hounding of Lawyer Glidewell, who well may have coached Alma to use what had worked so well against his own cross-examination of Pardue.

Taking another tack, the solicitor seemed half-kidding and half-serious when he commented on her many newspaper pictures and asked if she hadn't come from jail smiling for the photographer the other day.

Attorney Glidewell asked the court to rule against this line of testimony; but the examination was over. The defense had no redirect questions to ask.

Among the many character witnesses introduced were: Mr. and Mrs. Francis Womack, W. F. Gant, Will McCollum, W. G. Lowry, W. T. Moore, Miss Myrtle Moore, Faison Smith, D. A. Price, W. J. Mitchell, J. W. Michael, E. G. (Pete) Sacrinty, W. A. Stanley, Dr. J. R. Meador, Mrs. Meador, R. L. Holmes, and Miss Fuchia Dockery. All gave Alma a good name.

Douglas Butler, a fourteen-year-old employee of Pender's Grocery, told the court that Mr. Pardue told him he might as well tell the truth, since he would have to tell what he knew. But Doug didn't tell them everything he knew.

He didn't tell them what he had belatedly realized about the significance of the half-ton of coal ordered from Newell's Coal Yard: He should have known at the time that there was something fishy going on when he found his buddy Woodrow in the basement moving part of the coal pile to a nearby spot. When he'd asked the older boy what he was doing, he said he was shoveling coal, what did it look like he was doing? "Good exercise, builds your muscles up," Woodrow said. "Want to shovel some?"

So Douglas had unwittingly helped Woodrow cover Mr. Petty's secret grave with the coal that had missed the murderer's intended mark.

Another witness, Mrs. L. M. Swanson, was not as outgoing as her husband, who was well known for his smart-aleck humor. He ran a fruit stand and had once told a customer who asked him if he kept Winesap apples: "No, madam, I don't keep 'em, I sell 'em." Mrs. Swanson was brief and to the point when she took the stand and said that Pardue had asked her if she ever knew Alma to take a drink, and that he would like to have her help him out.

Mrs. J. S. Turner testified the minister wanted her to tell him what she knew about him, that he had sold a little whiskey before he was converted.

When Woodrow Wilson Petty took the stand that afternoon, his testimony was a carbon copy of his sister Alma's story: the father's drunken homecoming, his attack on Woodrow's mother and sister, his own running up the back steps and into the kitchen with the ax that his mother used to kill his abusive daddy; every detail repeated verbatim. The same contradictions, the same denials. And the boy even laughed at the same place in the testimony where Alma had laughed.

But Woodrow was too pat, causing a number of people in the courtroom to wonder if either his or Alma's story was anything more than a skillful performance delivered from a memorized script.

The jury, however, did not appear to see any of it as theatrics, especially not Alma's occasional tears during her testimony. Indeed, more than one of the jurymen had been observed shedding a tear along with Alma when her voice broke at the mention of her dead mother's name.

Impressed by P. W. Glidewell with how important his testimony would be in their determination to save his sister from the electric chair, Woodrow may have learned his piece too well. But all the work put in by both the boy and the defense to make sure he was ready must have seemed worthwhile after Woodrow weathered the state's cross-examination with as much aplomb as a well-coached high school debater.

Although Judge Cameron MacRae had announced that he would hold court until six o'clock, at 3:45 court was unexpectedly adjourned until 9:30 Monday morning.

19

I don't remember whether my brother Nathan went to the Petty trial or not. He was almost sixteen, so he may have gone. But I'm not sure, which is not too surprising when one considers how selective memory is. A good example: I have no recollection of my father's being foreman of the Grand Jury which brought a true bill to indict Alma Petty Gatlin for the murder of her father. It was a complete surprise to me when I learned about it while doing research in old issues of *The Reidsville Review;* though I can't imagine my not knowing it at the time and being proud because my daddy was the foreman. On the other hand, my being there when they dug up Mr. Petty is something I will never forget. Such is the fickle nature of the selectivity of memory.

I can say with absolute certainty that I didn't go to the trial a single time. I know I would remember it if I had been there, with everything that was going on in that overcrowded courtroom; my memory couldn't be that selective.

I know for sure that Mama didn't go either, because she stayed home with my invalid brother Vernon and with Grandma, who was real sick. But the whole family kept up with the trial in the newspapers. Just about everybody in town read every word printed in the newspapers about the trial; whether they had been lucky enough to be there or not, they still wanted to see how it was written up in the papers.

Sometimes we'd get first-hand reports from my brother Buck, or Daddy. But they couldn't go every day; though Daddy was required by law to be in court on the designated day that he and his partner in the drugstore, T. Lytt Gardner, along with about fifty other Reidsville residents, were summoned as witnesses for the defense. Daddy said he didn't hear anybody complaining about being called; he guessed they all were glad to get a guaranteed seat at the sensational trial.

On the days Daddy did go, he would come home full of what he'd seen and heard at the courthouse and entertain us at the supper table by imitating Porter Graves' slow and deliberate way of talking. When he quoted something Graves had said, Daddy would affect one of his little mannerisms and slowly stroke his fingers one by one, the way the solicitor did when he talked, measuring each word.

I can't remember any of the specific details that Daddy told us about the actual prosecution, but I can still see the way Daddy's blue eyes twinkled when he did his impression of Porter Graves, a man he plainly admired.

I didn't learn until I was grown that Daddy had known him in Mt. Airy, where Mama and Daddy were married in 1899, two days after Christmas.

Daddy said when Alma's brother Woodrow took the stand as a witness for the defense, he handled himself extremely well for a boy not yet sixteen.

Since I never saw Woodrow in a courtroom setting, when I think of him, what I see is a freckled-faced neighborhood boy who was always grinning. Probably the reason I remember his grin so well is because his teeth always looked dingy. Brushing your teeth twice a day was something Mama always stressed when I was growing up, and I'm sure that was what made me aware of the condition of Woodrow's teeth, which looked almost brown to me. Chewing tobacco could have been the culprit, though I don't remember ever noticing him spitting a dark stream of tobacco juice like the baseball players on the Reidsville Luckies team did. When I wanted to act big, I used to chew the bitter curly leaves of rabbit tobacco that we kids gathered in the fall from fields and vacant lots where it grew wild. I would pretend I was chewing Penn's Natural Leaf, but I never tried the real thing.

Something else I remember about Woodrow Petty is his chipped front tooth, which gave him a sort of snaggle-toothed grin. I had never thought of it until I began searching my memory, trying to get a picture of how Woodrow had looked when we were neighbors. It occurred to me that here was a boy with dingy teeth and a chipped front tooth, but it didn't seem to bother him at all, since he was always grinning. Perhaps, what he was saying was: this is the way I am and that's it. Could have been a kind of Huck Finn attitude. Since he was three years older than I was, I never really knew him well enough to say.

Ike Truitt recalled sixty-five years later that his father had brought Woodrow home to stay with them a while and Woodrow said, "They found a dead man in the basement and they said it was my daddy." Ike said that he had never forgotten what Woodrow told them. To me, Woodrow's words had the plaintive ring of a lost boy.

My memory of Woodrow's little brother, nine-year-old Smith Petty, is vague. I don't recall any distinguishing features. His being a little small for his age is about all I remember about how he looked. But I have never forgotten how Smith became the proud owner of a brand-new bicycle.

After Alma moved the family from their Lindsey Street residence, Smith transferred to Lawsonville Avenue School, where Miss Nell Frashure, a member of the faculty, spent forty-six of her fifty years as a teacher. She was ninety-six years old when she sadly recalled how the other children playing on the schoolground seemed to shun the boy after his sister was put in jail pending her trial for murder.

Made to feel like an outsider, Smith could hardly wait to get the bicycle he had been promised, so he could ride it across the tracks and show it off to the kids in his old neighborhood, especially his friend G. W. Windsor. All of us were impressed and when somebody asked where he had gotten the new bicycle, he replied, "From Mr. Glidewell. Got it for learning my piece. But I didn't have to say it."

Smith's older brother Woodrow didn't get a bicycle "for learning his piece," but he did get written up in at least one newspaper as "a good-looking boy, who was a wonder, the way he spoke his piece so well." He was too good, some thought, obviously convinced that Woodrow Petty had memorized Alma's version of how the murder was committed and who the actual killer was.

Many courtroom spectators were in total agreement with Attorney Gwyn when he told the jury that Woodrow had "crossed every 't' and dotted every 'i.'" But it wasn't up to the visitors; the twelve men in the jury box were the ones who had to decide what the truth was. The spectators could only return home and speculate on the outcome of the trial or perhaps chuckle over the story making the rounds about Woodrow's teacher's getting after him because his grades were falling off, and somebody said the reason Woodrow wasn't making good grades was that he had been putting all his time on memorizing his speech instead of studying his lessons.

20

Monday morning's court session was largely taken up in debating the admissibility of evidence.

Just before the noon recess, Les Cain took the witness stand. Through the testimony of the manager of Belk-Stevens, the store where the deceased mother of the defendant had worked, the defense proposed to show that Janie Petty was absent from her work on the day that Alma said her mother had killed her father with an ax.

On cross-examination, the prosecution asked Cain whether he had personally made out the records he referred to in his testimony. The witness said that as manager of the store, his duties did not include making out the payroll. He admitted that he didn't remember whether Mrs. Petty had worked the day in question or not and explained that all he could do was go by what the records showed.

Will R. Dalton, associate prosecuting counsel, quickly turned to the jury and smiled a triumphant I-told-you-so smile.

It was more than P. W. Glidewell could stand. He jumped to his feet and made a passionate plea against "this man Dalton's continually smiling and smirking during this trial, and influencing the jury in that manner." The state attorneys, Glidewell contended, were making a game out of the trial.

Glidewell was known to have a volatile temper, as he had demonstrated the previous week when he angrily shook his fist at Pardue's supporters, after they had applauded the preacher when "he got ole P. W. told," as one of Pardue's church members later described the incident.

This time, it was Will Dalton's grin that finally got the best of

Glidewell. Every day it had aggravated him a little more, the way Dalton kept smiling every time he caught his eye, as if he knew something that Glidewell didn't know. It had been going on ever since Porter Graves' sore throat made him decide to call on Lawyer Dalton to help with the state's speeches. Glidewell wasn't feeling too well himself and he was getting madder and madder at the way Dalton kept grinning like a Cheshire cat, even when the defense was making a convincing argument. And if he wasn't grinning, he would fake an expression of trying to contain his amusement and not burst out laughing.

What had brought the situation to a head was when Glidewell angrily declared that the prosecution had from the outset of the case deliberately tried to influence the jury by Dalton's persistent grinning.

The effect of Glidewell's accusation was instantaneous: Dalton's grin vanished and he quickly rose his feet with some hot words. Porter Graves stood and solemnly jumped into the quarrel.

Saying not one word, Judge MacRae sat looking at the three lawyers. The court could not rule on the Dalton smile until the argument subsided. His face still red, Glidewell got control of himself and waited while Dalton and Graves protested simultaneously. Within a minute or so, they stopped talking as suddenly as they had begun and the three lawyers, still standing, waited for the judge to break the silence.

Judge MacRae ruled that Dalton had the right to smile. "If Mister Dalton can see anything to smile or to smirk at, I suppose he is entitled to smile and smirk at the jury and at the court," the judge concluded.

Chagrined, Glidewell didn't dare to even glance at his nemesis, because he knew he would see that satisfied smirk. He knew something else: Will Dalton didn't look anything like Will Rogers. That was just something one of those city slicker newspaper writers cooked up.

In the early afternoon, when Will Dalton opened for the state, his solemn expression was a perfect match for the tone of his remarks.

"If I were not speaking to men who believe in Almighty God and in His Christian ministry," the forty-three-year-old lawyer said quietly to the jurors, "I would know that the story of the Reverend Mr. Pardue would have no effect. I would know that the state's case would make no appeal to you.

"But I know that you believe him, as a minister of God, when he stated that this girl had confessed the murder of her father to him;

that she had told him that for two years she had had a pistol with which she intended to kill her father.

"I know that you do not credit her story that she had lied to him there in the presence of God because she wanted to shield her mother, who was then dead. That's a fine kind of mother love. Trying to foist her crime on her dead mother.

"The defense tried to keep out his testimony because, they said, a confession of this sort was inviolable and could not be told in court.

"They tried to show that the minister had done it for publicity. But I ask you what else could a reasonable and law-abiding man have done? If he had concealed it and it had come out some other way, don't you think he would have been implicated as an accomplice?"

Shaking her head from time to time in denial of some of his statements, Alma took her eyes off Dalton only when she looked down at her pad, taking notes as he spoke. She stopped writing, her green pencil poised above the pad, and stared angrily at him when he attacked her good faith in telling the story of her mother's death, when she said she had begged her mother to confess the killing.

Defense Attorney A. W. Dunn, who followed Dalton, began his speech with a bitter denunciation of Pardue, who appeared more gaunt than usual as he sat gazing attentively though impassively at the lawyer who declared in a loud voice that the evangelist was a "Judas, unworthy of his profession."

Dunn held the preacher up to public shame as "one who had violated inherent age-old religious teachings by breaking faith with and betraying a person who had made a confession to him." The lawyer even chastised the minister for delivering two sermons at his new church on Sunday "while Alma Gatlin waited in the shadow of gallows in her jail cell where his charges had put her."

Dunn finally got down to the facts of the case and while contending that Pardue's version of Alma's story was impossible, he reviewed the evidence as presented by the defense and said that it was "the most natural thing in the world for Alma to defend the memory of her mother, even at the risk of involving herself." He then declared that "the remainder of the testimony of the defense bore out the contention of the accused that Mrs. Petty killed her husband and swore her family to secrecy, which was not even released at death."

Dunn stressed that the jury should keep in mind that Alma

had told Pardue that the body of her father was carried away in a Dodge sedan.

"That is what she claimed her mother had told her, and at that time she was simply repeating what she had been told and was ignorant of the fact that her father had been buried in the cellar," Dunn concluded, satisfied that he had made a good point for the defense.

Dalton's argument for conviction had taken an hour and five minutes, while Dunn had spoken an hour and three-quarters.

The light was fading fast from the cold, gray February sky when Judge MacRae declared court adjourned until Tuesday morning.

21

When court convened at 9:30 Tuesday, F. Eugene Hester opened with the summation for the defense. With the immediacy of a determined prizefighter responding to the bell, the bald-headed barrister pelted Pardue with names like sensationalist, emotional preacher and sly deceiver.

The evangelist had taken advantage of his position, the lawyer scornfully declared, and deceived the youthful defendant, then betrayed her confidence when she went to him and made a "hypothetical confession" in an effort to learn whether her mother's soul could be saved.

Hester spoke at length to discredit the preacher and destroy his account of the confession. He also sought to show that the state had presented no evidence to prove the guilt of the defendant.

"It is a question of a man's reputation or a woman's life. This man persecuted and prosecuted Mrs. Gatlin in order to save his own reputation," Hester declared. He concluded his summation by reminding the jury that he was not asking for anything other than simple justice for the defendant. "She is entitled to it at your hands. We have not asked for mercy because we were not seeking it, but in your deliberations, temper justice with mercy and we have no fear of the result."

The day's first speaker for the state was handsome Special Prosecutor Allen H. Gwyn, whose lifetime achievements would include serving two terms as a state senator before going on to be elected a judge of the North Carolina Superior Court. During his career on the bench, which would span thirty-one years, he was to become widely known and respected for his concern with penal reform. A book he would write called "Work, Earn and Save" would become a guide for programs modeled on his work-release system aimed toward the rehabilitation of first-offenders.

A little more than five months earlier, the Caswell County native had been acclaimed in the press for the important part he played as Rockingham Solicitor in the investigation which led to the discovery of the murdered man's body and the arrest of Alma Petty Gatlin, who now sat listening attentively to every word of Gwyn's opening remarks.

The state pointed out that the defense had shown no inclination to dwell on Alma's testimony and he would show why: It was because "the testimony of Mrs. Gatlin would not bear the close scrutiny that fact will stand."

The thirty-four-year-old prosecutor had other corroborating facts that he could not present to the jury, because his special investigation on August 31 was unofficial and the people questioned had testified of their own free will and were not under oath. Since the people who appeared at Gwyn's unofficial hearing had not been sworn, the best he could do was to hint at answers given at that time, which were at variance with sworn testimony of witnesses on the stand.

When Gwyn solenmly declared that the state intended to bring no charge unfair to Alma, his sincerity so impressed the defendant that she burst into tears, the first of a number of times she was to cry.

Alma cried for several minutes when Gwyn described her dying mother and declared that Alma had tried to force a false confession from her. But the most dramatic reaction from the defendant was to come at the conclusion of Gwyn's powerful argument to the jury. After stating that Alma's version of the killing was "thin air," he asked that she be convicted of first-degree murder, calling for the death penalty in the slaying of her father. Upon hearing this, Alma broke down, shaking with uncontrollable sobs.

Point by point, Gwyn built his argument that Alma's story on the stand was not reasonable; and after each fallacy was presented, he would quietly declare, "It's too thin, gentlemen; that won't do."

He said that it was unreasonable that Alma could have been stunned after her father struck her with a stool and then failed to ever mention or to show that it made a mark.

He noted Alma's minute description of her father's bringing into her mother's bedroom the bucket of coal in one hand and the knife and ice pick in the other, setting the coal down and then turning on the light. He wondered aloud how Alma could see all that detail if the light were out.

He facetiously called attention to Alma's remarkable powers of observation while fighting for her life. She reported in minute detail what happened in the kitchen and what her mother and her brother said as her father was choking the life out of her with one hand and his other hand was raised over her with a butcher knife in it.

He called attention to the position of the major fractures in Petty's skull as described by the physicians and declared they could not have been inflicted by a blow from the rear as described by Alma on the stand, but were evidently delivered when Petty was sitting down and given with a blow from the side.

He pointed out that Alma and her brother Woodrow had given identical accounts of the killing from start to finish; identical statements of what everybody said, how everybody acted. Gwyn asked why this one time such a detailed description was possible unless they had conferred and agreed upon the account.

The defense was afraid to put Alma's sister Thelma and her cousin Annie Reedy on the stand, Gwyn said, because their stories might not match up with Alma's and Woodrow's.

"Why do they withhold this precious stuff for which you are yearning," he asked the jury, referring to the evidence that Thelma Petty and Annie Reedy could give if the defense had let them.

Gwyn said Alma was looking out for her own interest, rather than her mother's soul, when she pleaded with her dying mother to confess; and Alma's anxiety and grief were over her own safety.

"When Alma went to Pardue," Gwyn said, "she had no reason to be worried over her mother's salvation, since she knew her mother had acted in self-defense, commendably protecting her daughter when she struck the blows she says her mother struck."

Gwyn denounced the defense's attacks on Pardue as prejudicial and declared that they "had raked the minister's record with a fine-toothed comb, but had been able to find aught against him...other than the fact that he had had his automobile painted and not finished paying the bill."

"They have gone back over Mister Pardue's life from the cradle to the present day and that was the sum of his iniquity that they could bring here," Gwyn said.

In spite of defense's efforts, they could not prove that the preacher had tampered with a single defense witness and his reputation remained above reproach.

As proof that Pardue had told the truth about his interview with Alma Petty Gatlin, Gwyn called attention to the fact that Smith Petty was found in his grave in a position indicating that he had been doubled up in a trunk as Alma had told him. Also, the body was wrapped in blankets as Alma had told the preacher he was wrapped.

Gwyn declared that the facts announced by Pardue before the discovery of the body and which were substantiated when the body was found had forced the defense to adapt its presentation of the case to fit the facts. "It forced them to rouse old Smith Petty at 5:30 a.m., leave him clad only in his underclothes and his shoes and keep him that way for two hours or more on a cold January morning, with but a blanket thrown over his shoulders, in order to fit in their story with the established facts of the story Alma told Pardue."

Defense Attorney P. T. Stiers, the first speaker of the afternoon, began by quoting medieval English laws that "held incompetent a confession made under stress of religious fervor;" and he cited several decisions to reinforce his argument. Then, speaking softly and slowly, he told the jury: "Counsel for the state have intimated that Mister Pardue, being a preacher, should be implicitly believed. I say that you should give the words of such a preacher no credence. That you should remember, when the state tells you that this man is God's representative, what God's greatest representative did over in Judea when they brought to him a woman charged with what was a capital offense in that country.

"Remember how he picked up no stone, but wrote his verdict in the sand so that it would not remain.

"There is another class of ministers of God and this man is of that class. There was Cotton Mather, a brilliant man who, though a minister, was so little a Christian that his persecution burned hundreds of witches. That's the kind of minister Pardue is. A witch-burning Judas," he said stridently.

"A witch burner because he would love to see this innocent girl die. A Judas because he betrayed her when she came to him in the name of Christ.

"A Judas in that he has made this betrayal for mercenary reasons. Ah, gentlemen, how I wish you could see that man taking up a collection in his church.

"How I wish you could see him, a sensational and emotional preacher of admitted power, dragging confessions from the hearts of those that came in repentance."

The state objected at this point that this was not in the evidence, and Judge MacRae sustained the objection.

Stiers nodded almost imperceptibly and explained, "I only want to bring out to you that it is ridiculous to intimate, as the state has intimated, that Pardue made himself the prosecutor in this case because he feared that he would be implicated as an accomplice after the fact if it came out some other way and because it hurt his Christian conscience that Alma's father did not have a Christian burial. He could not have been indicted as an accomplice, as he did not either aid or abet the crime.

"Gentlemen, this girl is on trial for her life, but more than the life of a good girl is on trial here. On trial before you is the name of North Carolina and religious liberty and the right to confess our secret sorrows and to ask for guidance from those from whom we should receive that guidance.

"If you do not bring in a verdict of not guilty, this case will go down in history as one of the greatest setbacks to freedom and decency that has been recorded in our history."

When court adjourned until 9:30 Wednesday morning, Attorneys Hester, Gwyn and Stiers had argued for a total of about five hours.

22

For several days, P. W. Glidewell had been feeling that he was coming down with something and his indisposition had been compounded Tuesday night when he'd had a bad attack of indigestion.

Now, with the big day at hand, he was feeling worse and running a fever as well. Afraid he might have the flu, he knew he should be home in bed, but he refused to give up. He meant to plead Alma's case. And he did, eloquently, as all his friends and admirers were to agree.

He enjoyed their praise, but saved for a privileged few the explanation of how a man as sick as he had been was able to bring it off with such style. The story was to become one of his favorites in his extensive repertoire.

Many years after the trial, Glidewell told a younger lawyer about it. And with Glidewell long since dead, the lawyer recently passed the tale along to me.

Glidewell's good friend, T. Jeff Penn, brother of millionaire Charlie Penn and himself a millionaire who ran a dairy farm for fun, had brought the attorney a quart fruit jar of top-grade bootleg white liquor, so smooth it didn't need a chaser.

Just before court convened, Glidewell took a couple of generous swigs of the corn whiskey, ostensibly for his flu. And as he was later to describe the combined effects of his fever and the booze, after that everything was just one big blur and he didn't remember a word he had said in his speech to the jury.

But high or not, Glidewell was a spellbinder, equally impressive in the courtroom, over a poker table, or teaching a Sunday school class.

A few minutes after court convened, Glidewell began a speech in which he would instinctively balance substance with style, further enhancing his already considerable reputation as a colorful criminal lawyer.

He quietly related to the jury how Alma had turned in her hour of trouble to the very man who had become her prosecutor: Rev. Pardue. Suddenly raising his voice, Glidewell said sternly, "His friends and adherents have applauded him here in her hour of misery."

Allen Gwyn quickly voiced an objection to using the term "adherents." But Glidewell, seeming to take no notice, continued his speech.

"I delight in the opportunity to defend this girl," he said, "after many good friends have turned against her."

He described the defendant as suffering the handicap of being "born of a drunken and dissolute father;" so she had no choice save to quit school at sixteen and take a job "in order to help her poor mother put food in the mouths of the family -- a family that lived in a home where this father brutally mistreated her mother.

"When this thing happened in her home, they did not call the police. They hid the skeleton in the closet, unwilling to place it before the gaze of the world.

"Many women are that way. They shield themselves from the hurt of the world. And then last March, she saw her mother die from a broken heart, ill and miserable from the cruelty of a drunken father.

"She had seen her mother kill her father. Then she saw her mother die. Then that poor girl looked out upon the world alone, without a friend -- the head of the family.

"She turned to a man who called himself a man — a man who betrayed her confidence. You heard her tell him from this witness chair: 'Mister Pardue, I had more confidence in you than in any man in the world when my mother died.'

"He claims to be an ambassador of God and this girl in her misery turned to him. In her own words, she said, 'His God was my God and his religion was my religion. I joined his evangelical band. I followed him to Winston-Salem and Reidsville, where he held meetings. I had confidence in him.'"

Turning to the state's attorneys and pointing at them, Glidewell continued: "And when she sat down in this witness chair in defense of her life on charges for which this man is responsible, they knew he was a prosecutor and crouched him behind them in front of the girl who had trusted him, so that he might prompt them in their cross-examination."

Glidewell then retold to the jury the story of how the girl had gone to the evangelist with her confession and how he, after telling it to the police, went back for more details.

"He asked her, this loathsome murderess, to come to his house for supper. Was there ever a more enticing scheme devised?

"Why did he ask her to go there? To get her soul right with God, so when he got her killed in the electric chair, the soul might go to Heaven. Did he pray? Yes, he thanked God for himself."

Addressing the state's declaration that they had tried to be fair to the defendant, he said, "What you do speaks so loud I can't hear what you say."

Later, he argued that every part of the evidence came from Alma herself, and that it would be unjust to take part of what she said and use that against her, while rejecting another part.

"I ask you to believe what she says here under oath, rather than take what this preacher says she told him."

Glidewell then ridiculed that part of Pardue's testimony where he said that Alma told him she sat on the body of her father and talked with him.

"The doctor testified either blow would have killed him," he said.

"Strip the case of everything that came out of her mouth and you have nothing but the body." He then rebuked Pardue by declaring: "She asked for bread and he gave her a stone. He betrayed her, misconstrued her and became her prosecutor."

A few moments later, Glidewell was telling the jury that never before had he been so interested in a case, but he was unable to speak as he wanted to, because he was still in pain from an attack of acute indigestion he'd had during the night.

"But I'm willing to spend every ounce of my strength in this defendant's behalf," he said resolutely. "The eyes of the nation are on this case, because the people of this nation think the preacher did not give this twenty-one-year-old girl a square deal."

He then pleaded for a verdict of either first degree murder or freedom for the girl, explaining that if Pardue was to be believed, then it was murder in the first degree. "But if you believed her, it is freedom.

Under the evidence, you can't convict her of first degree murder."

Warning the jurors not to be swayed by the eloquence of Solicitor Graves, he begged them to give the prisoner the benefit of reasonable doubt and turn her loose.

Next, Glidewell began to paint a picture of what would happen if the girl were found guilty. He described her trip to the electric chair, her death and the return of the body to "little Woodrow and little Smith."

He chose to forget that "little Woodrow" was approaching sixteen and had done a masterful job just last Saturday reciting his almost identical version of Alma's testimony. A lot of the spectators must have forgotten, too, for Glidewell's vivid description had many in the courtroom weeping along with Alma and her brothers and sister.

"There is no blemish or scar on this girl's spotless character, which is as pure as the driven snow," Glidewell said. "God knows what has passed through my heart since I took this case five months ago. I have served without one cent of compensation and I declare to you that to be her spokesman here today is the proudest moment of my twenty-five years as a lawyer," he said, concluding his speech that had lasted more than two hours.

A short recess was taken prior to the prosecutor's summation.

At his wife's insistence, Solicitor Graves had spent Sunday in bed, recuperating from his severe cold of the previous week. Without losing a day in court, he appeared much improved on Monday and by Wednesday he seemed his old assured self again.

Graves took the floor at 11:40. At first, his voice was unnaturally low and husky; but it soon cleared up and gave him no further trouble, although he would speak for more than three hours, with time out for lunch.

The solicitor began his speech by vigorously ridiculing the testimony offered by the defense and declared that the reference to the electric chair was an unfortunate attempt to gain the jurors' sympathy.

"Truth is the guiding star to you in your deliberation," he said. "The reason I point this out is that the state has been accused so often of clamoring for human blood.

"The counsel has told you that the multitude would acclaim a verdict of not guilty. Great God! The acclaim of the multitude! Do your duty, gentlemen, and refrain from thoughts of the multitude."

Graves pointed out that no one had been brought to the stand to testify to the bad character of Smith Petty. "Nobody," he said, "except the two members of the murdered man's own family, has been here to say he was cruel."

He reminded the jury that Glidewell said that when a client employed him, he advised this client "as to the best thing to be done."

"Great God!" Graves shouted in exasperated disgust, causing laughter to ripple through the courtroom.

Judge MacRae rapped his gavel for order and sternly threatened to jail anyone who laughed again.

"Honestly," the solicitor continued, "isn't it enough to make angels weep? Every man of you who weighs the testimony feels that her story is the smoothest ever told. It ran like a book.

"Ah, I advise you of the best thing to be done, and thus it fits," Graves said derisively. Then he read part of Alma's testimony and followed it by reading part of her brother Woodrow's testimony, pointing out that "even the phraseology was similar."

As brilliant as the wellborn solicitor was, he didn't seem to know how, if indeed it occurred to him, to reduce his language to the level of the common man. The observation previously made by Allen Gwyn that Woodrow had "dotted every 'i' and crossed every 't'" was a better way to make the point that Alma's brother had memorized her version of the confession.

Graves had been speaking for more than an hour when court adjourned for lunch.

When court reconvened at 2:15, Graves took the defense to task for attacking Rev. Pardue, "a good man who had done what he thought was right."

"Gentlemen of the jury, the defense has taken a strange position," he said. "They abuse him for betraying a confidence. They say he is a liar and that he told what was given to him by a penitent. Why abuse him if it is not the truth? They spend more time denouncing him than they do arguing that the defendant didn't do it."

Reviewing the testimony, the solicitor characterized Alma's story of her father's assault as pure fabrication, impossibly full of holes. He made his point by asking: "If a man weighing nearly two hundred pounds had hit his daughter with a stool, why wasn't she injured?"

The defense's evidence dovetailed too neatly, he said, adding that if Alma, swayed by Pardue's emotional preaching, told him after his sermon that she murdered her father, there was little chance of its being a lie.

To show proof that Alma had confessed to the preacher the same facts that he related in his testimony, the solicitor described the posture of Smith Petty's body in the grave: doubled-up in the shape one would assume it to be after being in a trunk, where Alma had said he was first placed.

Another point stressed by Graves was the presence of the round hole in the skull. It was the kind of hole that would result from a blow with a piece of galvanized iron pipe, which was what Alma had used to finish her father off after she discarded the ax, according to the preacher's testimony of Alma's confession.

Going into many other points at great length, the solicitor took the jury on an emotional roller coaster ride, his delivery running the gamut from whispering to shouting and waving his arms.

Concluding his closing argument for the state at 4:30, Graves had good reason to feel that he had been at his dramatic best. All he could do now was wait and see what the jury decided. But it would be another two hours before the judge finished his charge and instructions to the jury.

Addressing the jury, Judge Cameron MacRae stressed that the court held that the case hinged on the credence placed in Pardue. If the jury believed him, it must be a first degree verdict, and if it did not believe him, it must be an acquittal.

Then, as required under North Carolina law, the judge read the testimony of sixty-two witnesses, going exhaustively into the evidence of Pardue and the accused woman, before concluding with summaries of the defense's case and the state's case.

At 6:32 the judge finished his charge and sent the jurors to their supper with instructions to return immediately after their meal for deliberations.

23

Packed all day with a record-breaking crowd, the courtroom had dwindled at almost 9:30 that night to little more than a shell of its former surging self.

Late in the afternoon, spectators had begun trickling out as the judge droned on and on with his ponderous charge. When he finally finished and sent the jurors to their supper before they were to begin their deliberations, the mention of supper triggered a mass exodus of hungry and tired spectators, leaving the courtroom half empty by 6:45. And during the next two hours, many more people who had to go to work early the next morning reluctantly went home.

A couple of dozen or so die-hard spectators still loitered about. They had missed their supper and stayed on, hoping that a verdict would be returned before midnight. If the jury reached no verdict by then, the word was that the judge would order the jurors to their rooms at the Belvedere Hotel in Reidsville.

Alma's husband, her siblings and cousin Annie Reedy were keeping a vigil in the defendant's jail cell across the road from the courthouse. Time seemed to drag by and Alma was worried that things weren't going right. Her family tried to encourage her. Everything was going to come out all right; she'd see, they said.

Her attorneys had already told her that in the unlikely event that the jury should convict her, she was still not to worry, because they would simply file an appeal. And if it came to that, they felt sure that the Pardue testimony would be stricken by a higher court.

Comforting words, but not necessarily true. The thought of

what could happen still frightened her.

When they heard the metallic echo of footfalls on the iron steps, everybody in the accused woman's cell stopped talking at once, waiting to see if it was who they all were hoping it would be. And it was indeed the kindly jailer, Mr. Irving. He unlocked the metal door and told them what they had been so anxious to hear: The jury was ready to report.

"It won't be long now," Alma said, trying to sound lighthearted.

The news spread like wildfire and soon it was all over town that the jury had agreed and that Judge MacRae had already left Reidsville and was on his way to Wentworth to take the verdict.

The moment they got the word, fifteen newspapermen, who had been so busy writing their stories they hadn't taken time to eat supper, dropped everything and dashed out of the Belvedere Hotel. The time had come and the mad race round bad curves in the pouring rain was on.

The courthouse blazed with light, a beacon for the racing reporters and speeding spectators. Unmindful of dangerously slick roads, they were determined to make it to Wentworth in time to hear the jury announce its verdict.

Hurrying into the courtroom, the reporters found Alma and her family already seated beside the counsel tables. Her four lawyers waited nearby. Slouched in a chair, Eugene Hester appeared lost in thought, while A. W. Dunn wandered about aimlessly,

P.T. Stiers, another of Alma's four defense attorneys. (Photo courtesy Sara R. Hopper)

speaking with apparent nervousness to first one spectator then another. Pale-faced P. W. Glidewell, who had positioned his chair so he would see the faces of the jurors the instant they came out, tried to hide his nervousness by puffing on a cigar. P. T. Stiers gazed with heavy-lidded eyes at Alma until he caught her attention and became the only defense attorney who had an optimistic smile for her.

The low hum of conversations quickly faded away at the appearance of Judge MacRae in the doorway of the anteroom. His expression emotionless, he slowly climbed the platform steps, then settled in the large chair behind the bench and watched reporters and spectators rise from their seats while Chief Deputy Sheriff Dick Stokes chanted "Oyez, oyez, oyez," announcing that court was in session. There were no more than a hundred and fifty people outside the railing.

Judge MacRae gave the stern warning that he would tolerate no demonstrations of any kind in his court and instructed the deputies to bring before him anyone who did not heed his warning.

Her hands folded in her lap, Alma sat looking toward the jury room as the judge instructed Deputy Sheriff L. W. Worsham to bring the jurors in. Watching the deputy fumble in his pocket, the defendant blinked nervously and shuddered when he produced the key, unlocked the door and disappeared inside the jury room.

Seconds later, Alma watched the jurors come out and walk in solemn single file toward the jury box. She studied the face of each man as he stiffly took his seat. But their fixed expressions told her nothing.

"Stand up, Alma Gatlin," said Major Smith, the clerk of the court.

Flanked by her sister Thelma on her left side and her brother Woodrow on her right, Alma arose, struggling to appear calm.

The clerk of the court continued, "Defendant, look upon the jury; jury look upon the prisoner. How say you?"

Alma steeled herself. But instead of the verdict, she heard only a confusion of voices as several of the jurors began talking all at the same time.

"Which one of you is the spokesman?" the clerk asked patiently.

W. M. Carter stood up and stated that he was the foreman.

"How say you?" Major Smith said.

The foreman, one of the two store clerks on the jury, answered in a clear voice. "Not guilty," he said firmly. It was ten minutes past ten o'clock.

The verdict electrified the courtroom, setting off a buzz of excitement. Reminiscent of the sound of swarming bees, the hum of voices leveled off and died down as suddenly as it had begun. No explosive reaction, hence no gavel pounding.

Judge MacRae, his hand on the gavel, watched Alma sway for an instant as her face went deathly white. "Thank God!" she exclaimed, as P. W. Glidewell reached out to steady her before she fell sobbing into the arms of her husband.

"You can take your wife home, Mister Gatlin," said Judge MacRae.

Woodrow Petty, who had managed to hide his feelings through much of the trial with his chin cupped in his hand, heard the verdict, stared at his sister, and sucked in a deep, shaky breath. Suddenly he was sobbing. He heard not one of the judge's kind words to Alma's husband.

P. T. Stiers' shoulders shook as he slumped forward in his chair. Emotionally exhausted, he covered his face with his hands, while P. W. Glidewell beamed happily, delighted to be the first to take Alma's hand, which he vigorously pumped with great relish.

Glidewell answered the request of one of the jurors, who asked if they might shake hands with Alma, by calling her to the box, where the discharged jury still lingered.

Tears streaming down her cheeks, she took the hands thrust at her from both sides, unable to speak as she made her way toward the jury.

"Why, you ought to be smiling," said the first juror to shake Alma's hand, whereupon Glidewell grabbed Alma's sister Thelma and gave her a big kiss, bringing a surprised smile to her tear-stained face.

As Alma shook hands with each juror, most proudly made the claim that they had never doubted her innocence after they had heard her story.

A considerable crowd of people anxious to shake Alma's hand and wish her well had gathered about her and she shook hands with as many as she could reach while slowly making her way toward the bench. When she reached Judge MacRae, he smiled down at her and shook her hand as she expressed her simple thanks.

The reaction of the spectators made it obvious that they approved the jury's verdict. But not everybody was happy. Though they tried to hide it, disappointment was written on the faces of the three attorneys for the state who sat at their table silently watching Alma as she shook more hands before starting toward the door with P. W. Glidewell and her husband. Trailing them, Woodrow Petty couldn't stop grinning, now that it was all over and his sister had been set free.

Before Alma reached the door, she found herself facing Solicitor Graves, who had left his seat. Instantly in control, she extended her hand and smiled faintly as she thanked him. She told the prosecutor that she knew he had a duty to perform and she wanted him to know that she had no bitterness over it. His smiling reply was a courteous thank you, delivered with characteristic courtliness.

While the rest of Alma's family crossed the road in the cold downpour and went into the jail with her, Woodrow ignored the rain as he hunted for the car they came in. He was "plumb worn out" and planned to "sleep all day tomorrow."

The only things Alma picked up from her cell were her hat and a curling iron; the rest of her stuff could wait until tomorrow. With her husband's arm around her waist, she emerged laughing and talking. They were so elated that neither gave a thought to P. W. Glidewell's vow of several months ago that he would drive Alma back to Reidsville on the front seat of his car, a free woman. Although the lawyer would have been as good as his word, he was too delighted with his victory to worry about Eugene Gatlin's forgetting about the bargain and driving his wife home himself.

In all the joyous excitement, it never occurred to any of them that for the first time since the trial began ten days ago, missing that rainy night was the man who had started it all: Rev. Thomas F. Pardue.

24

I t had been almost five months since Rev. Pardue's dream of having his own church to do the Lord's work had become a reality.

His congregation wanted to name it Pardue's Tabernacle; but the preacher convinced them to name it Lawsonville Avenue Baptist Church. Facing Montgomery Street, the modest new frame building was about half a mile from Greenview Cemetery, where Smith Petty and his wife lay buried side by side in graves that would remain unmarked seventy-five years later.

It had gladdened the preacher's heart when the foundation for his first little wooden tabernacle was laid by a "converted infidel," since "saving lost souls" was the work that God had called him to do. And he had begun a revival on the opening day of his new church on Sunday afternoon, October 2, 1927, with services to be held each night at 7:30.

On Tuesday night, the evangelist based his message on "the thought of a real revival of the old time religion in the hearts of men and women," according to *The Reidsville Review*, which said that "the message so stirred the audience that at the close, an invitation was given for all to come for prayer who felt lost, and many came, with some falling down on their knees at the altar crying aloud for mercy and pardon, confessing their sins which brought victory to their souls."

By Thursday night, Pardue's church had added eighteen new members to its roll. Under the preacher's enthusiastic leadership, the Lawsonville Avenue Baptist Church continued to grow and would reach a membership of nearly two hundred within ten months of the time it was organized on May 20, 1927.

In a letter that appeared in *The Reidsville Review* on March 21, 1928, Pardue thanked "fine spirited citizens" for light fixtures "paid for with money made up outside the membership of his church." Without mentioning names, he also thanked a local man for a forty-odd pound ham and a farmer for a bag of flour, and said that never in his life had he had more good substantial people to encourage him by word and act than he'd had for the past several weeks. His letter went on to say: "I am a happy man with a definite call from my church to remain pastor for an unlimited time, more people coming to hear me preach than we can seat, new members every week, and with unlimited possibilities for us, we shall, under the direction of our victorious Christ, go forward. Unshaken in my determination, I say to the people of Reidsville and Rockingham County that I am here with you to see the dream of my life come true."

Pardue was already dreaming of replacing the little frame building with a modern brick church, "an edifice," he wrote, "able to accommodate the multitudes that are coming each Sunday knocking for entrance at our packed tabernacle, many having to turn away for lack of room."

It is possible that many in his congregation thought the preacher had gotten carried away and his grandiose plans to build a big new church would cost more than they could afford; and they didn't see any sense in biting off more than they could chew. Some disenchanted members may even have made up their minds that the preacher had lost his humility and was getting too big for his britches.

Although Pardue had expressed great happiness with his church in a letter published in *The Review* just a little over a year earlier, the preacher was to resign his pastorate after serving only two years. And a short time later he and his family would move away. Whether he ever returned to Reidsville is not known.

On the last day of the trial, before he left the courthouse while the jury was out, Pardue had told a reporter for the *Danville Bee* that he still felt he did his duty. "It has been hard to suffer the unkind things said about me during the trial, but that was part of the burden. Far from being a prosecutor, I have the deepest sympathy for this young woman." And he had been impressively adamant when he declared, "It is my intention never to speak of this thing again nor to refer to it."

But, as reported in the *Madison Messenger* on September 5, 1929, the preacher failed to live up to his announced good intentions: "Tom Pardue, an alleged minister of the gospel went on a rampage at a mill village in Greensboro the other night and re-enacted the Gatlin murder case. He also paid his respects, if he possesses such, to the newspaper and officials of Reidsville...He even went so far, according to the *Greensboro News*, as to tell the congregation that he had a pistol in his automobile and would use it with deadly effect if anyone attempted to molest him. He also told his congregation that he had been working all his life for nothing."

While the trial was in progress, an anonymous caller had telephoned Pardue at his home about midnight and said, "You'd better clear out or we're coming down there and 'git' you."

Questioned about the threatening call, the preacher had insisted to a reporter from *The Reidsville Review* that he was "not alarmed in the least, for I am sittin' pretty if they come." The reporter asked "if his home was armed." Pardue answered that was his own affair. "But if they come, I'm sittin' pretty," he reiterated.

The preacher didn't like the way the newspapers had "played him up and got their facts wrong half the time." And though he had spoken to the reporter with bravado, he may have been more upset by the threat than he cared to admit.

The Reidsville Review reported on February 24, "It became known today that one day during the trial Judge Cameron MacRae received by some means a note severely denouncing Rev. Thomas F. Pardue for having given away the purported confession of Mrs. Alma Petty Gatlin." Though the paper did not say so, the note was undoubtedly not signed and added more emotional weight to the anonymous telephone call, which may have been preying on the preacher's mind, causing him to make the statement over eighteen months later that he would shoot anybody who tried to molest him. However, understanding what might have made him tell the congregation such a thing makes his actions no less strange, especially when one considers that he was a minister.

In May of 1930, Pardue was back in the news again when he allegedly tried to kiss the seventeen-year-old daughter of the pastor who invited the evangelist to hold a revival at the Flat Rock Baptist

Church in Mount Airy, the hometown of S. Porter Graves, the solicitor who prosecuted the Gatlin Case.

According to the *Winston-Salem Journal*, Pardue was classed about those parts as "a minister of the Holy Roller type and gets credit for going the limit with the emotional phase of religion; so far to the extreme does he carry it that many people do not care to even participate with him in his services." Many in the congregation were sorry that their pastor, Rev. A. L. Harrison, had wanted Pardue, but rather than divide the church, they had not made an issue of it. However, after all the bad publicity, they wished they had acted on their opposition.

It was already being whispered about by some in the congregation when the *Mount Airy News* reported that the local preacher's daughter, Myrtle Harrison, said "Pardue offered to take her home from a service but instead drove her in his automobile into the country and there made advances to her."

Pardue called on the church members for a hearing, which he dramatically advertised as a "trial." He admitted that he asked for a kiss, was refused, and that was as far as it went. Through a series of questions asked by Pardue and answered by the girl, the accused preacher established that he had neither offended nor insulted her in any way. Her father, Rev. Harrison, then "made a very strong appeal to all to drop the matter and have no further discussion, declaring that he and all his family were satisfied and held nothing whatever against Mr. Pardue. Then, before all the congregation, he gave Mr. Pardue his hand, assuring him that the matter was satisfactorily settled and that their faith and confidence were still in him."

Although a statement signed by the deacons of the church said that "Myrtle Harrison, together with the entire congregation, also walked down (the aisle), giving the same assurance," the church was divided in their opinions of Pardue. A few hours after the "trial" was over, it was "decided that the circumstances justified the church in taking action to close the meeting and not permit the services to continue longer."

Under the headline "Red Hot On The Trail Of Pardue," *The Reidsville Review* included stories that had appeared in the *Winston-Salem Journal* and the *Mount Airy News*. An excerpt follows:

"One citizen who was at the last meeting and saw the whole performance staged tells us that part of the defense put up by Mr. Pardue was to recount how the men of old as recorded in the Old Testament were able to have many wives, some to live in adultery with the wife of another man and yet (have) the favor of the Most High. Vividly he contrasted his own conduct with that of the holy men of old. After all this, he got down on his knees and in a most dramatic way prayed long and loud, and so excited did he become that he finally got down on his 'all fours' and crawled about in the dust of the floor weeping and carrying on like a man beside himself. Part of what he was saying while down in the dust was to beg the Lord to forgive him. To say the least, it was a sight that those who beheld it would not soon forget."

The brick building that Pardue had dreamed of was to become a reality about six years after he left Reidsville. Completed in the summer of 1935, under the leadership of Rev. D. W. Overby, and renamed Penn Memorial Baptist Church, the new building occupied the same spot where Pardue's Tabernacle once had stood.

Seeking information for a history of her church, Estelle Martin interviewed Pardue in Winston-Salem in the mid-1960s and found that age and illness had dulled the flashing eyes that once bespoke the theatricality of the fiery, young Thunderbolt Tom Pardue.

The retired preacher was seventy-five when he died at Baptist Hospital on October 26,1966. They took him back home to Yadkin County and buried him in the Oak Grove Baptist Church cemetery, surrounded by the beloved rolling hills of his childhood.

A man ahead of his time, had Pardue been born in the '40s or '50s, he surely would have capitalized on his flair for histrionics to become a highly visible television evangelist raking in millions, instead of "working all his life for nothing," as he often said in his declining years.

25

"I've lied like a dog to you the past five months," John W. Irving, the jailer, confessed to reporters the day after the trial ended. He said that when he was telling them that Alma was "always cheerful and in such fine spirits," the truth was that "all during those long months she had suffered the tortures of hellfire."

Having lost forty pounds while she was incarcerated, Alma did not look like the same round-faced girl that Irving had locked in her cell on September 3. But she was in high spirits after her release in February when she talked to a *Reidsville Review* reporter and told him how happy she was to be home again.

"Yes, it's true," she said, "I've received some very attractive offers to go on the stage and be in the movies, but I've not decided what I'm going to do. I am conferring with my attorneys, Mister Glidewell and Mister Stiers, and may reach some decision within the next few days."

Nothing was to come of the offers to go into show business, and Alma would leave Reidsville in the fall, moving with her husband and their new baby to Greensboro, where she was to find work at the Blue Bell overall plant. A big comedown from fairy tale offers of appearances on the stage and screen to the reality of a job in an overall factory.

Eugene Gatlin would take a job as a film operator, and by 1929 Alma would be employed as a clerk with Mock, Judson Voehringer Company, a hosiery manufacturer. The couple eventually moved to High Point and Lola Neal Preddy recalled selling tickets as a young woman at that city's Broadway Theater where Gatlin worked in the projection booth.

The day after Alma was found not guilty, she told a *Review* reporter that she knew the jury would believe her story. "I never once thought there would be a miscarriage of justice," she said. "But sometimes there was an awful unexplainable fear of the electric chair. Just suppose..."

The *Review* also quoted Alma as saying she credited a lucky penny, carried in her shoe during the trial, with her escape from the electric chair.

But the general consensus was that luck had nothing to do with the jury's verdict of not guilty. What saved the accused girl was her unwavering refusal from the moment of her arrest to make a statement. Had she taken the stand at the coroner's inquest and told the story she told at her trial, the state would have known what to expect, with the added advantage of ample time to prepare a solid case aimed at damaging her credibility. But by following her counsel's plan to keep the state guessing what her version would be, she succeeded in making her story less vulnerable when it came out in her testimony.

— Defense's strategy had worked, and on February 24 *The Reidsville Review* reported that the paper had learned that "most of the members of the jury had virtually made up their minds on the case before they entered the jury room, maintaining an attitude of 'mental open-mindedness' (sic) until the last words of the judge's charge reached them."

In the same story, the newspaper also stated, "It was said the jury took only two ballots. The first was ten to two for acquittal, but the two jurors soon changed to the ten's decision."

One week later, the *Review* ran without comment the following single paragraph: "'In arriving at a decision in the Gatlin murder trial at Wentworth the jury took only one ballot, the twelve men all voting for acquittal of the defendant, Mrs. Gatlin, on the first ballot,' says T. R. Simpson, of near Summerfield. 'There was no division of opinion among the jury when the vote was taken and counted,' declared this juror."

Certainly the clearest and probably the most accurate report appeared in the February 23 issue of *The Danville Bee*: "On the first (ballot), ten (jurors) stood for acquittal and two for first-degree murder. These two men did not understand the judge's instructions, and when they were explained to them, they came over readily."

Would a different verdict have been reached had a Reidsville man realized before the trial began the importance of his observations and gone to Solicitor Gwyn with the same information he gave me? Everything the man told me is included in the vignette which follows:

The twenty-one-year-old young man had the same tall, slender build as his father, for whom he worked in the watch shop which occupied one side of Bolyn Harness Shop, with no partition between the two businesses. The father fitted glasses and kept a small stock of jewelry and pocket watches. Both father and son repaired watches.

Sixty-five years later, the son recalled the day Alma Petty came into the shop dressed in the white nurse's uniform she wore at work. She handed him a metal syringe that Dr. Meador wanted soldered, so he could continue to use it in his dental practice.

The young man noticed Alma's finger was bandaged but thought nothing of it at the time. But something clicked eight months later, when he read the account in the *Greensboro Daily Record* of the confession that Rev. Pardue alleged Alma Petty had made to him. One of the things the preacher quoted Alma as saying was that after she had hit her father in the head with an ax, she knelt beside him and put her hand over his mouth so the neighbors wouldn't hear his groaning. The dying man bit her fingernail off and scratched her hand hard enough to make it bleed; so she had to wear a bandage several days.

Reading about it, the young man decided at that moment that the preacher was telling the truth. How could he doubt it? He'd seen the bandage with his own eyes.

He was young and the cold wintry air hadn't bothered him as he drove his open Ford car past the Petty house on Lindsey Street. But what did bother him, and puzzle him as well, was the smell of burning cloth which stung his nose.

Continuing to read the preacher's version of the confession, something else dawned on the young man: What he had smelled last winter must have been Alma's and her father's blood-soaked clothes being burned. That was the way Alma said she had gotten rid of them, according to Rev. Pardue's sworn statement. Now the young man was even more convinced that the preacher was telling the truth.

There was another smell, one that the young man grown old said he could never forget. It was the terrible stench he had smelled that Saturday when he was heading toward the west end, on his way home for lunch — called dinner in those days. He had seen a crowd in the Petty yard and known at once what they were doing there — he'd heard about the decomposed body in the basement just as he was leaving the shop.

He said he didn't stop. Never saw the body. Never wanted to.

A few days after Alma's acquittal on February 22, a big victory party was held at the home of P. W. Glidewell. With food and drink in abundance, hosts and guests were all surely in high spirits as they celebrated the winning of Alma's freedom.

When he heard about the party, Sheriff Chunk Smith's comment was that it sounded like they had a Belshazzar's Feast. Knox Lively, a scholarly Reidsville man who had been a student at the University of North Carolina when Thomas Wolfe was a big-man-on-campus there, said he liked Chunk Smith and he was a good fellow but he couldn't help noticing the sheriff's mispronunciation of the biblical word when he used a long "a."

Belshazzar's Feast or not, it turned out to be quite a party for P. W. Glidewell, and many years later he took obvious pleasure in recalling what had made it so special for him. Stressing that Alma's sister Thelma was the pretty one, P. W. let his considerable ego take over and, according to one of his friends, bragged that Thelma approached him and said she wanted to thank him for the wonderful job he did convincing the jury to set her sister free, and before the night was over he said he had received "the finest fee he ever got."

Some time later, Attorney Eugene Hester was to complain to a lady who worked downtown that he never got a nickel for helping defend Alma, only to be told by the outspoken woman that she was glad of it.

EPILOGUE

About a month after the trial was over, Alma's younger brother, Smith, was driven to Oxford Orphanage in Charlie Barnett's Buick with Thelma Petty at the wheel. Young Smith would spend almost three and a half years at the orphanage before leaving in August, 1931, to stay with Alma at 300 Willowbrook Street in High Point where she and her family were living at the time.

In 1939, a former schoolmate at Oxford Orphanage spoke to Smith in Mann's O'Henry Drug Store in Greensboro, where he was working on the soda fountain. A few years later, Smith reportedly was driving a cab in Washington, D. C. and was said to have eventually moved to California.

Listed as a textile worker, Woodrow W. Petty's name appeared in Greensboro city directories from 1930 through 1939. Beyond that time, he was not listed in either Greensboro or High Point directories, leading to the assumption that either he had moved to another city or had died.

A search of Guilford County Courthouse records by genealogist Corinne Murray produced the answer: Woodrow died in Greensboro on February 27, 1969. Separated from his wife, he had died of chronic alcoholism at the age of 56 in Moses H. Cone Hospital.

It was hard to find out much about Alma's years in High Point. But I did learn from a local resident that Alma's religion extended well beyond her mere presence in a church pew every Sunday. She studied the Bible assiduously and was often invited to speak at church circle meetings.

I don't know what prompted the Gatlins' eventual decision to leave High Point. It could have been the prospect of better jobs to be found somewhere else, or perhaps Alma wanted to distance herself from piedmont North Carolina, escape her unwanted notoriety, put the bad memories behind her and make a fresh start. For whatever reasons, Alma and her family did move in 1935 to a pleasant town in another southern state, where she surely found contentment, for it was there that the Gatlin family would put down roots.

Eugene Gatlin loved children and many of the neighborhood kids seemed to think more of him than their own fathers, who didn't take up as much time with them as Gene did. He was always playing ball with them when he wasn't working.

Gatlin was a movie projectionist in the same town for sixteen years before he died in 1952, survived by his wife and three children: two married daughters and a son, a student who still lived at home.

When Alma, who had been busy being a wife and mother, found herself a widow at 45 with no job and one child still at home, she knew exactly what to do. She got down on her knees and asked the Lord to help her; and her prayer was answered.

Alma was a good cook and she went to work at a boarding house. The Lord continued to bless her and within ten years she had two boarding houses of her own. She expanded into the rest home business and eventually was taking care of over one hundred patients housed in several residences.

Careful with her money, she kept her eyes open for good real estate buys. She invested and she prospered, always insisting it was the Lord who had done it. It wasn't her, she said, it was the Lord who made all those good things happen to her; and she couldn't stop praising His name.

Every once in a while, even after all these years, talk among Reidsville area residents will turn to a discussion of the town's most famous crime. And the question unfailingly asked is: What do you reckon ever happened to Alma Petty? The answer may come from different quarters, but in essence it is always the same: What they'd always heard was that when Alma left Reidsville she went to High Point but that was years and years ago and she was bound to be dead by now.

It was this kind of thinking that made my friend G. W. Windsor and me so sure that nobody in the world would have ever believed it could happen. Indeed, we had trouble believing it ourselves. Yet there we were, on a sunny Tuesday afternoon, the first day of September, 1992, sitting in Alma Petty Gatlin's living room. We were a long way from Reidsville, but the trip was worth it: the search was ended and the riddle of what happened to Alma was about to be answered.

G. W. had waited beside me while I knocked on the front door of an attractive one-and-a-half-story brick house. In less than a minute the door was opened by a pleasant woman who lived with Alma and appeared to be in her late seventies. I gave the lady our names, told her where we were from, and asked if we might speak to Mrs. Gatlin concerning the whereabouts of her brother Smith, who had been G. W.'s childhood playmate in Reidsville.

Alma, who had celebrated her eighty-sixth birthday on the previous Sunday, heard the conversation and came to the door, immediately inviting us to please come in.

Uncertain earlier about how we might be received, we had figured we would be lucky if we got to stand on her front stoop and talk for even a couple of minutes to the infamous Alma Petty Gatlin.

We had also considered the possibility of the occupant's telling us that she was Alma Gatlin all right, but she was not the Alma Gatlin we were looking for. She did not tell us that, but if she had, it would have been the truth, because Alma Petty Gatlin, the accused murderess, was not to be found in that house. Or anywhere else. For, as we were soon to learn, the Alma Petty Gatlin who had been tried for patricide and found not guilty was gone forever. God's love and forgiveness had taken care of that.

As we chatted with Alma in her comfortable living room, G. W. and I were not long in realizing that the kindly lady who made us feel so welcome was not the same person who had the whole town talking sixty five years ago. And it was much more than the simple fact of her having grown old; she was an altogether different person.

The woman who sat facing us was someone we knew, yet did not know. But she was certainly not a stranger. Our conversation confirmed that she was indeed Alma Petty Gatlin, albeit a new Alma, one we had never seen before: A gracious Alma who radiated the joy of a true born-again Christian, a woman at peace with herself, one who loved the Lord and praised Him for giving her life new meaning.

During our visit that would last about an hour, we learned that G. W.'s boyhood friend had developed a drinking problem and died in California at the age of 47. Alma, who over the years had helped him financially, also provided his final resting place. On October 30, 1965, Smith Petty, Jr. was buried in the Gatlin family plot in the cemetery on the outskirts of town.

The next day, G. W. and I would visit the Gatlin plot where ground-level bronze markers lay at the heads of the graves of Alma's husband Eugene and his mother, Martha Stitt Gatlin. A check with the cemetery office would confirm that no marker was ever ordered for

Smith's grave, leaving little doubt that Alma did not want the Petty name to sully the Gatlin plot where she would eventually be buried beside her husband.

This evidence of her seeming aversion to the Petty name fit right in with what Alma had said in her home when she showed us a beautiful portrait of herself.

Taken in 1927 in his Reidsville studio by L. B. Throckmorton, the photograph made Alma look like a movie star and I told her so. What I didn't say was the black-and-white picture was a perfect example of why Throck was renowned among his peers as one of the best photographers in the state. A master of lighting, he was remarkable as well for his consistency in capturing good likenesses while successfully flattering his subjects. The man was indeed an artist with a camera.

Scribbled in pencil in the corner of the 8 x 10 print were the words "Alma Petty Gatlin" and underneath the name was a single word I couldn't make out until Alma said it was "Bratton," declaring it was a name she was proud of without elaborating further.

Careful to make no comment, I concluded this must be her mother's correct maiden name, erroneously listed as "Bracken" on the Xerox of her death certificate, obtained for me by county historian Bob Carter in the early months of my research. My conclusion was to be confirmed in a little over two weeks when G. W. and I made a trip to Fries, Virginia, where Alma was born. A suggestion from the local sheriff's office in the pleasant little town sent us to the home of an elderly lady. It proved to be a serendipitous meeting when we learned that the old lady's sister had married Tom Bratton, Mrs. Petty's brother and the uncle of whom Alma was inordinately fond.

Later, linking her pride in the Bratton name with the absence of a marker on Smith Petty, Jr.'s grave, G. W. and I agreed that undoubtedly the Petty name had become anathema for Alma, and she must have erased it from her memory bank along with all the unsettling episodes that the name conjured up. Those things were all in the past and indeed had no proper place in the new life that Alma Gatlin had long been leading as a born-again Christian.

Alma seemed genuinely glad that we had looked her up as she proclaimed her excitement over the opportunity to talk about old friends: Mrs. Pearl Leath, her beloved Sunday School teacher, Lula Shelton, who had married a preacher, Adrian Thompson, Reid Foster, who gave Alma a box of candy when they were just kids going to Lawsonville Avenue School, rosy-cheeked James Gardner who wore long sideburns and was her first love, Gene Gatlin's best friend and fellow fireman, Self Davis, who married Mary Lewis Kemp in a double-wedding ceremony with Alma and Gene, Cabel Davis who ran the Grand Theatre where Alma sold tickets. All dead and gone.

Among those still alive that Alma asked about was a person she said was one of her best friends. It would have been cruel to tell her that the woman had told me a few months earlier that she hadn't really known Alma very well; she was just somebody she would sometimes see walking past her house.

Alma smiled as she recalled the popularity contest that she and Elsie Benson had won, the prize being a sight-seeing tour of the western states which the two girls took together by train. I was glad to be able to report that Elsie and her husband James Thompson were both still alive, and the next thing I knew I was telling her the same success story that Mama had told me, about how James had started out as a trip boy for Gardner Drug Company, riding a bicycle all over town delivering medicine. He was a poor boy determined to make good and he did. He worked his way through pharmacy school at Carolina, wound up a registered druggist at the same drugstore where he'd carried trips as a boy, and eventually went into business for himself.

I told Alma that James had once said that people who paid attention to such things knew that if Chief Gene Gatlin wasn't at the firehouse, he was never far away and could usually be found at Gardner's, bellied up to the soda fountain, drinking a "dope." The nickname was Southern slang for Coca-Cola. Indeed, the original formula did contain cocaine from the coca leaves which were combined with kola nuts to give the drink its unique flavor.

Soon after the turn of the century, the Coca-Cola Company began having the coca leaves decocainized. But even without the cocaine, the soft drink still delivered quite a kick because of its high content of caffeine derived from both coca leaves and kola nuts. Neither tea nor coffee gave you the lift that "Co'Cola" did. Which explains why Gene Gatlin hit the soda fountain eight or ten times a day and drank two dopes, one right behind the other, every time he came in.

Once in the morning and again in the afternoon, before going back to the firehouse, the chief visited his fishing buddy, Charlie Tesh, whose business was next door to the drugstore. I had heard that Mr. Charlie thought so much of Gene that he had loaned him his car to visit Alma when she was in jail. But, of course, it wouldn't do to mention that to Alma.

Her mind still on Gardner Drug Company, Alma said she remembered it was close to the firehouse. But when I mentioned Ellington Drug Company, she couldn't remember it at all. Reminded that store owner Rucker Ellington's mother roomed at G. W. Windsor's house, just across the street from us, and taught piano lessons there, Alma didn't remember her or the Windsors either. Nor did she remember the Link family, although we lived just two houses away.

I wondered if it was her age or if she had blotted out my daddy's name because he was foreman of the Grand Jury that indicted her?

Hoping to jog Alma's memory, I reminded her that Ellington Drug Company was just down the street from the Grand Theatre where she and her sister Thelma both sold tickets. But she still shook her head no, professing she could not remember it.

I asked myself if it was because of a certain employee of Ellington Drug Company who had dated her sister Thelma and was rumored to be the man who had gotten Alma's mother pregnant. Reason enough to forget the drugstore and certainly the busy druggist.

I had heard that Thelma was dead, but I wanted to hear it from Alma. So I asked whatever happened to her pretty sister Thelma, immediately wishing I hadn't said it that way. She told me that Thelma had died in 1957. Woodrow was dead, too, Alma said, so she was the last one left.

When I told Alma that I had never forgotten what beautiful sparkling blue eyes her cousin Annie Reedy had, Alma was quick to let me know that although Thelma had been saved, Annie was bad.

Alma didn't mention that Annie was dead. But I already knew that she had died in West Palm Beach in 1980. Knowing she was terminally ill, Annie Reedy had contacted Pitt Wilkerson at the funeral home and made arrangements to be buried in Reidsville, where I had recently stood beside her grave in Reidlawn Cemetery. Feeling nothing for the sixty-nine-year-old woman in the ground, I could think only of the ebullient teenager she had been and see in my mind's eye those blue eyes that seemed to an eleven-year-old to dance with the excitement of being alive.

Because Annie Reedy was her sister Lizzie's daughter, Mrs. Petty had taken the child out of an orphanage, brought her to live with them when she was not quite thirteen and treated Annie Reedy like she was one of her own. Mrs. Petty didn't live to see how Annie Reedy would repay her aunt's kindness by stealing Thelma's millionaire husband while visiting the couple in Washington.

I hung onto every word that Alma spoke, not letting on that some time ago I had heard from Margaret Carter Cobb about Annie Reedy's running off with Thelma's husband.

Margaret, who had worked with Annie Reedy in a Reidsville beauty parlor in the late '30s and was familiar with her previous unhappy marriage to Sid Terry, said she still remembered what Annie Reedy wrote on the post card she sent her from Florida. Margaret recalled with a chuckle that Annie Reedy had written that she was "glad to know that you could be happy though married."

Alma told a different story; she said that the man who ran off to Florida with Annie never married her, concluding her remarks about the only person she'd had anything bad to say about.

When I stood up and said we didn't want to overstay our welcome, it was Alma's cue to say she didn't want us to get away without seeing her pictures. As we looked at each of the many photographs which hung in the hall and covered the wall beside the upstairs steps, G. W. and I came to the same conclusion and told Alma we could see why she was so proud of her progeny, all good-looking people, every last one of them, children, grandchildren and great-grandchildren.

After expressing sincere thanks for her hospitality, G. W. and I said our goodbyes to the warm and gracious lady who a lifetime ago had been the notorious Alma Petty.

Alma Petty Gatlin died Sunday, December 2, 2001. She was 95 years old.

The following is an excerpt from her obituary: "Mrs. Gatlin accepted the Lord as her Savior by grace through faith at age 26 and spent the rest of her life witnessing the wonder of the love of Jesus Christ. God richly blessed her life as she was an instrument for Him in the winning of souls.